A Dialogue Between East and West

Maria

I give you this book with
compassion, gratitude & respect
for taking care of my
children this weekend.

D
&
08·11·09

A leading educationalist, political thinker and economist, **Ricardo Díez-Hochleitner** was president of the Club of Rome between 1991 and 2000, and was active in leading positions at the World Bank, UNESCO and the Organization of American States. He has also served as vice-minister for education in Colombia and under-secretary of state for education and science in Spain.

Daisaku Ikeda is the president of Soka Gakkai International, a lay Buddhist organization with some eleven million adherents in over 190 countries throughout the world. He is the author of over 80 books on Buddhist themes and received the United Nations Peace Award in 1993. His work to restore Chinese–Japanese relations as well as his contributions to world peace, cultural exchange and education have been recognized by the world's academic community, which has awarded him more than 200 honorary academic degrees.

A Dialogue Between East and West

Looking to a Human Revolution

Ricardo Díez-Hochleitner
and Daisaku Ikeda

I.B. TAURIS
LONDON · NEW YORK

Published in 2008 by I.B.Tauris & Co Ltd
6 Salem Road, London W2 4BU
175 Fifth Avenue, New York NY 10010
www.ibtauris.com

In the United States of America and Canada
distributed by Palgrave Macmillan, a division of St Martin's Press
175 Fifth Avenue, New York NY 10010

ISBN: 978 1 84511 599 9 (HB)
        978 1 84511 600 2 (PB)

A full CIP record for this book is available from the British Library
A full CIP record is available from the Library of Congress

Library of Congress Catalog Card Number: available

Typeset by JCS Publishing Services, www.jcs-publishing.co.uk
Printed and bound in Great Britain by T J International Ltd,
Padstow,Cornwall

Contents

Illustrations

Preface by Ricardo Díez-Hochleitner

My respected dear friend Daisaku Ikeda, president of SGI, says in the text of this book: 'You from the West and I from the East must never stop urging the leaders of the world to engage in dialogue and cooperate in the name of harmonious coexistence.' In line with the above I have stated that 'The West must address the East face-to-face on an equal footing'.

In spite of different cultural roots and beliefs, we have shown in our dialogue how broad our common ground of understanding is, trying to serve the future of humanity and nature as well. Such was the spirit and scope of the earlier dialogue between Daisaku Ikeda and the first president of the Club of Rome, my admired and beloved colleague, Aurelio Peccei.

Instead of clashes of civilizations, we must aim for dialogue and cooperation, particularly in this time of growing uncertainty and anxiety throughout the world. Despite many important achievements in the past, and taking place now, in the present world there exists the root of the unease that is caused by the profound changes inherent in a transition towards a new global society and the threatened environment.

In this period of dramatic changes, there are breathtaking opportunities for freedom and wealth, but also immense risks for the future of the environment and the peaceful coexistence of people. The severe crisis in ethical and moral values within our social and political lives requires fundamental questions to be asked.

What some see as a great opportunity, others regard as a very serious threat; in these circumstances, the issues raised in the text of this dialogue will highlight the reasons for hope, provided we learn from leaders with a enlightened vision – such as the president of SGI – irrespective of our individual cultural identities, ideologies and beliefs.

We in the Club of Rome try to promote and provide opportunities for in-depth debates and discussions intended to contribute to a worldwide mutual understanding that is increasingly necessary.

Our main concern is to reach global agreement that will inspire local action, as well as local debates influencing global action. To this end, it is essential not only to define common ethical values, but ultimately to demonstrate cohesion between our words and our deeds.

Ricardo Díez-Hochleitner

Preface by Daisaku Ideka

I first met Dr Ricardo Díez-Hochleitner in June 1991, when he became president of the Club of Rome, the organization often referred to as 'the brains of humanity'. We were among those attending the opening ceremony of the Victor Hugo House of Literature in France. Dr Díez-Hochleitner is one of those courageous and distinguished intellectuals who are labouring to find solutions to the many global problems that confront the world today. At that time, he and I agreed at some future date to engage in dialogues that would lead to the production of a volume such as this. It was ten years or more, however, before we could begin our actual discussions; by making various adjustments in our busy schedules, and at times exchanging letters and drafts, we were nevertheless able to make satisfactory progress. The results of our work were serialized over about a year from May 2004 in the Japanese monthly periodical *Daisan Bunmei*. In the autumn of 2005 the Japanese text of the dialogues was published as a separate volume. The fact that the text is now to appear in English as well is a source of deep satisfaction to me. My most sincere thanks go to the British publisher I.B.Tauris & Co., and to all others who have helped to make its publication possible.

Dr Aurelio Peccei, the founder of the Club of Rome and a friend of both Dr Díez-Hochleitner and myself, in the course of discussions that he and I had, made the following observation about human history: humanity had already experienced three revolutions, the industrial, the scientific and the technological, all three of which were brought about by external forces. But he questioned both their goals and their implementations, arguing that our failure to develop the potential wisdom these revolutions could bestow resulted in surprising ignorance. While technology has advanced, culture has stood still, fossilized. He insisted that a human spiritual renaissance is essential to fill this gap. By this he meant a revolution of humanity itself.

In our discussions, both Dr Díez-Hochleitner and I have endeavoured to find some feasible way for humankind and the natural world to live in harmony. Together we have tried to discover how to attain a state of positive peace, one that renounces violence and seeks to ensure conditions of sustainable growth, coexistence between the human and natural worlds, and well-being for all individuals and ethnic groups in society, and to define the ethics and moral order upon which such conditions of positive peace can be based. Dr Díez-Hochleitner has contributed wisdom and many insights of traditional Western culture to the discussion, particularly based on the Christian spirit and cultural foundations of Spain. For my part, I have endeavoured to approach the problems from the standpoint of the spiritual and basic outlook of Eastern culture, especially that expressed in the Buddhist view of ethics, human existence and the natural world. To my profound delight, we seem to have succeeded in arriving at a deeper understanding of the values shared by all humanity, values common to both East and West.

Dr Díez-Hochleitner and I, like Dr Peccei, share the ideal of a 'human revolution', one that is founded upon the concept, common to both East and West, of the dignity of life. Such an ideal seeks to promote wisdom and understanding based upon love and compassion, with the importance of mutual respect, harmony with nature, and a global outlook. It aims for conditions of sustainable growth and positive peace, and hopes to achieve these through inner changes in individual human beings who will bravely carry out this mission.

In the period following the conclusion of the Second World War, in my opinion the person who most clearly perceived the need for such a human revolution was my mentor, Josei Toda. He took the lead in propounding the concept of the global ethnicity of all humanity, a forerunner of today's ideal of world citizenship. The global ethnicity of all humanity aims to go beyond narrow concepts of the individual and, while honouring the identity and specific characteristics of different ethnic groups, emphasizes the need to recognize the overall unity of all human beings of the world. These two ideals and concepts – human revolution and the global ethnicity of all humanity – are founded upon a system of values that recognizes the dignity of human life. Therefore, those who are capable of carrying out the human revolution are those that are true 'citizens of the world', the type of people needed to create a global civilization and culture.

An intellectual such as Dr Díez-Hochleitner represents such a model citizen of the world, and he has devoted himself to promoting the kind of education appropriate at this global level. He has expressed approval of our Soka University of America, which has as one of its aims the nurturing of such citizens of the world. Though the university is relatively small in scale and recent in its establishment, in May of 2005, at the very time when Dr Díez-Hochleitner and I concluded our discussions, the university sent its first graduating class out into the world. In our dialogues, as the reader will see, Dr Díez-Hochleitner and I have taken special care to emphasize the importance of education.

The people of the world today are starting more and more to tackle at a practical level the global problems that face us, particularly global warming and climate change. Training true citizens of the world and uniting with them in action, it seems to me, is the key to finding the way to a brighter future for humankind. It is my firm belief that when citizens of the world – men and women who are fully conscious of the dignity of human life – join together in action, they will be able to achieve true peace and prosperity for the world of the twenty-first century. I myself am determined to continue to do all within my power to realize that aim.

Daisaku Ikeda

ONE

Encounter with Aurelio Peccei

Ikeda: You once said, 'Tomorrow is too late. We must do something today. A sense of crisis drives my work because the problems humanity confronts are too big, too profound, and too urgent.' You went on to say that, though your contribution might be insignificant, you must think and act for the sake of humanity. The firm sense of responsibility reflected in those words inspired you to continue active work all over the world even after Prince Hassan of Jordan succeeded you as president of the Club of Rome. I am happy to be able to engage in dialogue with a person like you.

Díez-Hochleitner: I am the one who should be happy. Observing the way you travel around the world, I have wondered in amazement what keeps you going. I have only praise for your character, philosophy and work, and for the activities of Soka Gakkai International (SGI), the Buddhist organization you head.

I first heard of your work through your dialogue with my dear friend Aurelio Peccei. Discussions with you have been an extremely important spiritual and intellectual experience for me. They are at once an honour and a source of great inspiration.

Ikeda: I am grateful for your profound understanding of SGI. I first met you in France, in the Paris suburbs, in 1991 at the opening

1

ceremonies to open our Victor Hugo House of Literature. You had travelled from Spain for the occasion.

Díez-Hochleitner: Yes, I remember it well. The great writer Victor Hugo is of course very famous, but we Europeans have only recently started recognizing and respecting his true value in connection with the formation of the European Union. I had long entertained the idea of contributing to create a Hugo House but never thought the work would be accomplished by a single Japanese citizen.

Ikeda: In my youth, Hugo's literature was my companion and my very life; he fearlessly faced spiritual struggles. Today we are called upon to do the same. The Hugo House of Literature was created to continue his spiritual heritage and to be a citadel of culture, peace and human rights.

On hand for its opening ceremonies were Marcel Landowski, permanent secretary of the Académie des Beaux Arts; René Huyghe, art critic and member of the Institut de France; Kyrgyz author Chingiz T. Aitmatov; Pierre Hugo, a fifth-generation descendant of Victor Hugo; and Dr Serge Tolstoy, grandson of Leo Tolstoy. At the time, you and I decided to undertake a new dialogue to complement the one I shared with Aurelio Peccei, published in book form as *Before It Is Too Late*. We are now keeping our promise.

Díez-Hochleitner: I am sincerely honoured to be able to engage in a dialogue with you. I consider myself a disciple of Aurelio Peccei, founder of the Club of Rome. He told me how important his friendship with you was to him. Clearly, we of the Club of Rome share and are in accord with the philosophy and work of Soka Gakkai, irrespective of the very diverse cultural backgrounds and beliefs of our membership.

The Club of Rome can be said to have come into being because of Dr Peccei's concern over the future of humanity. Having survived the harsh struggle of the Fascist period after the Second World War, he was active as a businessman in China, Italy and Argentina. A humanist with great depth of personality and

2

insight, he sounded the alarm about the crisis careless human actions create in the natural environment. This immediately calls to mind your own profound philosophy of the need for humanity to live in harmony with nature; a belief and practice you both shared. For me, this has been a lesson of the greatest importance.

Ikeda: Dr Peccei's foresight is more illuminating today than ever before. He devotedly pursued the human revolution that is the *sine qua non* for all other revolutions. When did you first make friends with him?

Díez-Hochleitner: In 1964, when I was director of the department of investments in education at the World Bank. It was 'intellectual love' at first sight. I knew that he was a person I could love and respect as a brother and a friend. To achieve the ideal of contributing to humanity, I wanted to maintain lifelong ties with him. I knew this instantly.

In the early 1960s Peccei had expressed his concerns in a series of lectures and in a book entitled *The Chasm Ahead*.

In 1964, he was visiting Washington at the invitation of the then US Secretary of State Dean Rusk, and asked to meet me. Although still young, I had had undeserved opportunities and acquired an international reputation. Dr Peccei told me, 'You are internationally known as a great specialist with perspectives on future politics and educational reforms. What is your vision of society in the years to come? What hopes and possibilities do you foresee?' With his distinguished white hair and characteristically Italian gestures, he made an overwhelming impression on me.

At first, I thought he must be joking to address such questions to me. But I immediately understood that his innate sincerity prompted him to solicit my opinions, since expanding and improving education is a way of helping the future generations who will manage sustainable development.

Ikeda: Yes, I can almost hear his voice speaking in his sincere way. At the time, Dr Peccei provided the impetus that changed your life.

3

Díez-Hochleitner: Yes, he did. When and where did you first meet him?

Ikeda: Eager for me to engage in dialogues with leading intellectuals from all over the world, the British historian Arnold J. Toynbee gave me the names of several prospective dialogue partners. Dr Peccei's was one of them.

You say that your encounter with him was 'intellectual love' at first sight. I experienced an instant sympathy with his character.

He and I discussed revolutions in human nature and the human revolution, of which he himself was a real example. Of course, the nature of the human revolution depends on the individual. In the broad sense, it is the trajectory along which people either become better and create greater value within their own individual circumstances or move in the direction of attaining those goals. In the light of this definition of the human revolution, Dr Peccei, in my estimation, is a champion at inner-motivated reform and creation of value.

I sensed the unbending beliefs that had enabled him to survive Fascist oppression unbowed. Unclouded by personal interests or desires, his eyes saw far into the future, with a vision that was both long term and broadly inclusive. He strove to transcend specialization and embrace the interdisciplinary wisdom of the many. Looking reality in the face, he had the courage of his convictions and the will to put them into practice. At the heart of all this burned an ardent love and sense of responsibility for humanity.

He called the world leaders of the time irresponsible and argued that allowing prevailing conditions to continue unchecked would make the world of the twenty-first century a barren place and would ruin both nature and humanity. He blamed political leaders, businessmen, scientists, scholars and bureaucrats for doing nothing about glaring truths. He accused them of being confined to their own immediate interests and said humanity must undergo a revolution at once. I can still hear him saying with sincerity, 'There is no time left!'

Díez-Hochleitner: Certainly one of the great problems of today is the shortage of responsible leaders who realize that our crisis is more than purely material. The world now needs responsible leaders with a solid, long-term vision more than anything else.

Ikeda: The first of my five meetings with Dr Peccei took place on 16 May 1975. Although it was his wife Marisa's birthday, he came all the way from Italy to join me at our SGI centre in Paris. I was 47 at the time. At 66, he was a solidly built man, brimming with sincerity. Our meeting started in a reception room, but soon we left the confines of indoors for the garden and the blue skies of Paris in May. As we went outside, I was vividly impressed by his nimble movements and the smart appearance of a man who had spent years in the business community. Bright sunlight illuminated white apple blossoms and an orange parasol contrasted with the green lawn. Seats were carried outdoors, where we talked together for about two and a half hours.

Díez-Hochleitner: You paint a lovely word picture. How did your dialogue unfold?

Ikeda: Referring to human history, he said that humanity had already experienced three revolutions: the industrial, the scientific and the technological; all three of which were brought about by external forces. But he questioned their goals as well as their implementation. He argued that our failure to develop the potential wisdom these revolutions could bestow has resulted in surprising ignorance. While technology has advanced, culture has stood still, fossilized. He insisted that a human spiritual renaissance is essential to fill this gap. By this, he meant a revolution of humanity itself.

Until that time, he had advocated a humanistic revolution. But he finally agreed that, ultimately, everything comes back to the human revolution. He had a copy of the English edition of my book *The Human Revolution* with him. As we discussed these two kinds of revolutions, Dr Peccei asked how long it will take to accomplish the human revolution. He felt that the serious problems confronting humanity are too numerous for us to take

5

a century to re-form ourselves. I replied that, because it takes an individual about a decade, achieving the same thing for large groups is likely to require much longer. Still, we will make no progress unless we take action and sow the seed now.

Díez-Hochleitner: Dr Peccei used to say that under the sway of consumer lust, human beings waste natural resources and energy sources and in so doing are polluting the planet's soil, water and atmosphere. He also said that unless the future of the planet is taken into consideration, the natural environment, on which our existence depends, will be lost.

He believed that it is in our own interests to conserve and restore the environment. He also insisted that violating the natural environment is morally impermissible.

On the basis of future growth rates and population statistics in relation to natural resources, energy and the environment, the Club of Rome came to the conclusion that, while growth is important, it must be sustainable — the term 'sustainable growth' was not in use at the time. Our opinion was, if economic growth continued on the path it has followed thus far, the environment in which human beings live will be destroyed and the survival of humanity itself made impossible.

Ikeda: In his dialogue with me, Dr Peccei said the myth of economic growth has polluted the human mind. He warned of an approaching domino-effect catastrophe resulting from human population explosion, environmental destruction, squandering of natural resources and the tragic gap between the rich industrialized nations and the rest of the world. As idlers pleaded indifference or feigned to believe that things would somehow work themselves out, Dr Peccei shouted that the mistaken course of the errant ship of humanity must be changed at once. Otherwise it would be too late.

Feeling this way, in 1968, in Rome, he convened an intellectual conference that was the start of the global think tank called the Club of Rome.

Díez-Hochleitner: My relations with Dr Peccei deepened when I moved from Washington to UNESCO in France and then four years later to Spain. In Paris, we formed a small group of people, dissatisfied with our society and hoping to do something to improve it. Attending our small meetings were Alexander King, second president of the Club of Rome; my dear and respected friend, Mr René Maheu, who was then the director general of UNESCO; Mr Jermen Gvishiani, son-in-law of Soviet Premier Alexei N. Kosygin, and himself an important person in the Soviet Union; and Mr Hugo Thiemann, director of the Batelle Institute in Geneva.

In May 1968 I was appointed under-secretary of state for education, science and culture in Spain – thanks to the special, discreet support of Prince Juan Carlos of Spain (later King Juan Carlos I) – to direct a sweeping reform of Spanish education. Students in Western nations were organizing movements to voice their social dissatisfactions, and the occurrence of all these things in 1968 made me ecstatically happy. Although I actually took no part in the student movements, I realized we were being given extraordinary opportunities, thanks to their support for change.

Not believing in coincidence, I prefer to see this as a wonderful instance of cause and effect. It made me see reasons for my having been born. Things happen because they are supposed to. Perhaps I believe in providence. Be that as it may, I believe we must make use of all the opportunities life presents us.

Meanwhile, Aurelio Peccei convened a first formal meeting at the site of the Lincei Academy in Rome, which became in fact the formal starting point of the Club of Rome (CoR). The drafting of a first 'Report to the CoR' was entrusted to an Massachusetts Institute of Technology (MIT) research team, led by Donella Meadows, with the technical support of Professor Jay Forrester and the financial support of the Volkswagen Foundation.

Ikeda: And Dr Peccei was at the centre of it all, like a compassionate father figure. As a philosopher, he looked far into the future; as an economist, he was immediately decisive. Both these traits arose from his love of humanity – that was his greatness.

As you said, the Club of Rome could not have come into being without Dr Peccei's concern about the future of humanity. He is proof that a human revolution in a single individual can change the world.

In the early days, the mass media sneered at the Club of Rome. Dr Peccei was mocked as a prophet of destruction. But he remained a practical optimist who believed human beings can solve the problems confronting us since inner human confusion is the source of all the problems. The communists called him a capitalist; the capitalists called him a communist. People from the developing nations accused him of attempting to cramp their growth. Some irresponsible arguments claimed that the club's concern was like the fear eighteenth-century people felt: that increasing numbers of carriages on the road threatened to bury the world in horse manure. Some scholars ridiculed the club for ignoring technological advances.

In spite of all this, support for the opinions of the Club of Rome spread; today all humanity recognizes the limitations of our planet. Now, international organizations, national governments and private organizations everywhere are starting to deal with the global problems, the world's *problematique*. The United Nations Earth Summit of 1992 and the World Summit on Sustainable Development held in South Africa in 2002 represent such efforts.

We have sobered up from single-minded obsession with a richer way of life. The problem is immense, but the swell of international public opinion is stronger. Dr Peccei's one single step has grown into a giant leap for humanity.

He continued working actively until his death at the age of 75 on 14 March 1984. As a matter of fact, he was dictating a last testimony of his vision about the future from his sickbed until twelve hours before the end.

Díez-Hochleitner: In a way, this dialogue between you and me is a memorial to Dr Peccei. The living have the right and the responsibility to go on talking. But the dead, too — especially people like Dr Peccei, whose legacy survives for posterity — have the noble right to be remembered with respect.

Ikeda: I agree, and hope that honouring his noble right, and taking the philosophy and practice of the human revolution as our guiding light, you and I can discuss extensively the mission of humankind and the future of global civilization.

TWO

Childhood

Ikeda: According to our publishing department, this dialogue, which – in keeping with your suggestion – was entitled 'East and West, Eye to Eye' for the Japanese edition, is already stimulating considerable response because of its emphasis on peace and culture in the twenty-first century.

Díez-Hochleitner: I am very honoured. Being able to discuss diverse topics with you is a wonderful opportunity for thought, at a time when deep understanding between East and West is of the utmost importance.

Ikeda: You are truly a world citizen: you have been a member of the UNESCO executive board, secretary of state for education and science in Spain, director of education and planning in Colombia and head of the department of educational investment at the World Bank. I am very interested to know how you became such an active figure on the global stage. I understand that your father was Spanish and your mother German – the international nature of your family is indicated by the number of languages you all spoke: your father fourteen, your mother seven, and you yourself four.

Díez-Hochleitner: Yes, Spanish is the language I was educated in. Although we had few opportunities to speak German in my youth, I become comfortable with the language whenever I spend a few days in Germany. I use English and French in my work. I understand Russian (though was only fluent in it until the age of 10) and I still understand the literary structures of Latin and Greek.

My parents always honoured their respective cultural roots. Never parochial, they were very open-minded and tolerant towards cultural diversity. Brought up in this spirit, I grew up very aware of life's challenges and opportunities, and developed a strong mission to work in the area of progressive learning, reform and education. This approach together with a certain degree of audacity enabled me to grasp the many wonderful opportunities with enthusiasm and to develop them earnestly and with great passion.

Ikeda: Your mother and father were both linguists – I understand that your father compiled many dictionaries, among them an etymological dictionary of Spanish.

Díez-Hochleitner: I could talk about my father for hours; my heart swells at the thought of him. Born into a poor peasant family in Castile, he went to Bilbao, in the Basque region, to work and study. After specializing in philology, he received a doctorate in the sources of the Basque language. He taught in primary and middle schools before teaching at Deusto University and later at Salamanca University. Although he was greatly admired in Bilbao, he never put on airs. He was always deeply respectful towards his children, our mother and everyone else; he was a model husband and father.

Ikeda: You have inherited his magnanimous noble personality.

Díez-Hochleitner: He taught me that the most valuable thing is not material wealth but the acquisition of wisdom. He had no interest at all in material property. While praising scientific technology as a product of human wisdom, he made no use of it himself. He paid no attention to things like automobiles and could not even drive. His interest was always focused on reading and thinking; he received many scholarly honours. In 1971, in an academic ceremony, as vice-minister of education, I was privileged to present him with the Order of Alfonso X El Sabio award. I am at a loss for words to express the happiness I felt on that occasion.

He was also chairman of the Spanish Esperanto Association. He accomplished all these things because he was blessed in having had a splendid teacher in the person of Professor Ignacio Gejo, recipient of a State Award of Honour. In a provincial primary school, Gejo instructed my father up to the higher-education level, and taught him stenography and Esperanto.

Ikeda: The noble aim of Esperanto, which your father learned from Professor Gejo, is to unite all humanity.

Díez-Hochleitner: Yes. A Polish oculist named Ludwik Lejzer Zamenhof created Esperanto in 1887 by artificially combining elements from several languages. His wonderful idea was to produce a global tongue free of specific cultural references, psychological attitudes or considerations of profit. Esperanto was a starting point for my father's extensive professional involvement in philology. He wrote many books and translated numerous others from several languages.

Ikeda: Zamenhof was a Jew, born in 1859 in what is now Poland but was then part of the Russian Empire. He leaned towards Zionism in his youth but later abandoned it as narrow racism, in favour of what he called *homaranismo* or humanitarianism. The noble spirit of *homaranismo* is alive in you today. It was passed from Zamenhof to Professor Gejo, who transmitted it to your father, who handed it down to you. This kind of spiritual relay from mentor to pupil is always of the key to truly great people.

Zamenhof designated himself a human being and saw all humanity as one great family. Tsunesaburo Makiguchi, the first president of Soka Gakkai, considered himself a citizen of one world. Josei Toda, second president of Soka Gakkai, advocated

13

the global ethnicity of all humanity and always concerned himself with the future of the East and the Earth as a whole. As their heir, I strive to realize their philosophies.

Your father devoted himself completely to scholarly pursuits, but your mother must have been a great support for him. What kind of person was she?

Díez-Hochleitner: Like all mothers, my mother imparted love, tenderness and emotion, and engulfed us in warmth – she devoted her life passionately to her children. Born into an affluent Munich family with associations with the Bavarian royal family, she became one of my father's students at Deusto University in Bilbao. She was fourteen years his junior, and after studying philology she went to Spain to specialize in the Romance languages. There she met my father again and later became his indispensable assistant in the compilation of several dictionaries: for example, Spanish–German, Spanish–French, Spanish–English, and Spanish–Russian.

Both of my parents placed primary importance on their children's spontaneous freedom: after pointing out whatever we needed on a given subject, they left the rest completely up to us.

My father used to say he wanted to experience blindness; 'It must be a wonderful thing for deepening thought,' he said, 'because sight is so distracting.' Later he did in fact develop inoperable cataracts. He died at 92, holding my mother's hand as they spoke to each other for the last time. I have an inexhaustible store of memories like these.

Ikeda: A beautiful human drama. You speak four languages – what do you consider important for language learning? What did your parents teach you about it?

Díez-Hochleitner: First, it is best to start during childhood or youth. An environment overflowing with love is important because it facilitates language learning. As you pointed out, my father spoke fourteen languages. I was born when mother was learning Russian; she spoke it to me in my cradle, and the first words I uttered were in Russian. Next I learned German, my mother's native tongue. Although a Spaniard, I did not learn fluent Spanish until later, following French and English.

Father always worked hard to communicate his knowledge in the best way he could. My older sister and I spoke a different language each day of the week, so we might speak Latin one day and Greek the next. We were obliged to do so, but the request was imposed lovingly. Because they loved languages, Father and Mother always explained the etymologies and roots of words. We did not learn words as mere means of expression; instruction in them was accompanied by introductions to the admirable cultures they expressed. For example, together with the Russian language, we learned about Russian art and traditions and compared them with their Spanish counterparts.

Ikeda: Yes, learning a language is very important, though political conditions can hamper it. For example, in the militaristic Japan of my youth, English was forbidden as it was the language of the enemy. With prejudices of that kind, it is no wonder that our nation headed for destruction. Obviously we must keep an open mind and respect other cultures; a real citizen of the world suffers, rejoices and feels oneness and solidarity as a member of a single human race.

Díez-Hochleitner: The desire for mutual understanding provides a powerful impetus for linguistic study. We must strive to keep our minds open to other cultures, ideals and creeds. I have always challenged courageously whatever issues have arisen in my work. I have poured my whole soul into everything I have done, harnessing the forces of creativity, reform and imagination that are indispensable to linguistic improvement. Today this kind of imaginative power is called emotional intelligence (EQ), which is widely recognized as being highly important.

Ikeda: Linguistic learning must be an application of the whole human being in which full spiritual operations – emotional and intellectual — are mobilized.

Díez-Hochleitner: Yes. When he became advanced in years and I had already become very active internationally, my father suggested to me something that I have embraced as a fundamental truth. Because he wanted me to become a 'world citizen', he advised me to engage in dialogue with all kinds of people and told me to understand my own roots thoroughly in order to be able to understand other people's.

Even in the most hardened and limited realities, we can learn from and discern beauty in others. But understanding others requires us to know the basics about ourselves and examine our own good and bad points truthfully.

Ikeda: I agree. Examining our human elements is most important. Neither my mentor, Josei Toda, nor his mentor, Tsunesaburo Makiguchi, travelled outside Japan. As their disciple, I have travelled to fifty-four different countries and territories, where I have participated in discussions with many leaders. In this way I have ascertained the complete universality of the thoughts and actions of Mr Toda's and Mr Makiguchi's humanism.

Díez-Hochleitner: But now I should like to ask how a world citizen of your calibre came into being. I believe that Josei Toda played a major role in the process. I am interested in learning more about him.

Ikeda: You said your heart swelled at the very thought of your father. So too my heart swells at the memory of my mentor, Josei Toda. Ninety-eight per cent of what I am today I acquired from him. Born in Ishikawa Prefecture, he grew up in the fishing village of Atsuta in Hokkaido. Through the education system, he met Tsunesaburo Makiguchi, who became his mentor, just as Professor Ignacio Gejo became your father's. As students and seekers of human education, Mr Makiguchi and Mr Toda founded Soka Kyoiku Gakkai (Value-creating Educational Association), forerunner of Soka Gakkai.

Díez-Hochleitner: How did you come to meet Mr Toda? Why did you choose him as your lifelong mentor?

Ikeda: I met Mr Toda after the Second World War, in 1947, when I was 19. With the collapse of ultranationalism, the values of the Japanese people were in a state of total confusion. On one occasion, a friend invited me to attend a meeting where a philosophy of the very force of life itself was to be discussed. Because of my intense interest in the subject, and in Bergson's idea of the vital force, I agreed to attend.

Mr Toda was the speaker. Although Buddhism was his topic, he did not preach like a priest, nor did he indulge in abstruse word play like a philosopher. Instead he made keen observations in a liberal and open-minded way about practical life and the community. His personality was even more captivating than his words.

At the time, I had many questions about leading an upright life, true patriotism and attitudes toward the emperor. I put them to him, and his sincere replies went straight to the heart of each issue. Truths I had desperately sought suddenly became alive for me, and I understood that Mr Toda was a person I could trust. Now, when I reflect on the matter, I realize that Josei Toda's personality was a crystallization of the great wisdom of Buddhism.

Díez-Hochleitner: Wartime experiences must have influenced your decision greatly.

Ikeda: Of course they did. Both Mr Makiguchi and Mr Toda were persecuted and imprisoned by the military authorities for opposing their war of aggression. Mr Makiguchi died in prison; after two years of imprisonment, Mr Toda was released. These facts were decisive for me – I adopted as a measurement of character a person's strength to oppose war even when doing so meant imprisonment. Henry David Thoreau said, 'Under a government which imprisons any unjustly, the true place for a just man is also a prison.'[1] Both Mr Toda and Dr Peccei shone with a noble spiritual light because they endured prison in the name of their beliefs.

Díez-Hochleitner: I understand that Soka Gakkai philosophy holds that the reform of a single individual has great resonance for the reform of society as a whole. What was Mr Toda's source for this philosophy?

Ikeda: It came to him while he was struggling with life in prison. He said of those experiences,

> I was imprisoned for two years. It was hard but, thinking of it now, I see that I gained a lot from it. If I had not suffered in the darkness of prison life for two years, I would never have come into contact with Buddhism in all its greatness. I would not have acquired the supreme and noblest goal of life.

His courageous struggle with cruel oppression enabled him to dig down to the roots of his own self by making a thorough pursuit of the meaning of the Lotus Sutra, the supreme Buddhist scripture.

That pursuit made him aware of the universal force of life that, as the Lotus Sutra teaches, is the essence of life as manifested in each individual. Some people are aware of that force and dedicate themselves to embodying it and to trying to save humanity from suffering. The Lotus Sutra designates such people Bodhisattvas of the Earth. Mr Toda described efforts to embody this supremely worthy life force as the human revolution.

Released from prison and confronted by a war-ravaged nation, he had but one burning wish: to eliminate misery from the world. The basic way to achieve this is to help each individual accomplish his or her human revolution. Convinced of this he decided to rebuild Soka Gakkai and expand the human revolution movement.

Díez-Hochleitner: Consequently, I understand, you joined that movement and shared his hardships.

Ikeda: Under his tutelage, I received the best training possible. No matter how hard times got, I always considered studying with him the ultimate happiness. Two years after we met, I started working at his publishing firm. In the economic turmoil of the postwar period, his business endeavours faced bankruptcy; one by one, the other employees left, until I alone remained. Finally,

Mr Toda asked me to give up my night-school studies and do what I could to get his businesses back on their feet. In a tearful voice he apologized for changing all my plans. But I agreed at once. In exchange for my interrupted schooling, he taught me himself.

I attended what I call 'Toda University', and it was superior to all others. Until the year before his death, he lectured me on economics, law, government, chemistry, astronomy, the theory of life, Japanese history, world history and Chinese classical literature. The extra work this teaching schedule caused him may actually have shortened his life.

First and foremost, Mr Toda loved the ordinary people. He wanted to live in their midst, sharing their joys and sorrows as he spread Buddhist teachings. In this he embodies the attitude expressed by Nichiren: 'And Nichiren declares that the varied sufferings that all living beings undergo — all these are Nichiren's own sufferings.'[2]

At an early date, on the basis of the Buddhist spirit of compassion, Mr Toda urged people to consider themselves citizens of the whole world; that is, global citizens. In addition, he issued his Declaration for the Abolition of Nuclear Weapons and entrusted the task of accomplishing this ideal to the young people of the world. Soka Gakkai International (SGI) is now active in 190 nations and territories throughout the world. The goal of its peace movement is the realization of his ideal.

I am still profoundly grateful to Mr Toda and exalt him for his efforts to arouse in humanity the supremely worthy life force within each person. Doing so is my ultimate joy and my greatest mission.

THREE

Spain: Land and Culture

Ikeda: Now I should like to discuss the geography and culture of Spain, your homeland, and examine the spirituality of a nation that produces world citizens like you. Spain is known as the 'land of the sun' – what part of the country is most comfortable to live in?

Díez-Hochleitner: Well, the answer varies with the individual and mostly depends on whether friends, acquaintances or neighbours with whom one feels culturally and/or spiritually at ease are near by. Geographically, Spain has a great variety of landscapes, from its coasts to its mountainous centre; there are some climate differences but it is mainly warm. My favourite places, where I feel my roots are, are Bilbao and Palencia. Bilbao – where the award 'Honourary Consul' was bestowed upon me – is in the north; I was born and grew up there. It is an industrial city, with its characteristic foggy rain (*sirimiri*). Palencia, in the centre of Spain, is where my father was born and the place of which I became an 'adopted son'.

However, I also have fond memories of living in other places outside Spain: in particular Munich, Bogotá, Paris and Washington. Consequently, I feel in my heart and mind that I am not only a devoted Spaniard, but also a European and a world citizen,

21

thanks to frequent missions for international organizations across continents all around the world.

This feeling was enhanced by having honorary citizenship bestowed upon me by such countries as Tanzania, Afghanistan and, in particular, Colombia.

Ikeda: Your international experience accounts for your affection for these places.

Díez-Hochleitner: My wife is from Valladolid, near Palencia, in sunny Castile and Leon. After years of living abroad, when she and I returned to Palencia, I could not help exclaiming, 'Valladolid and Palencia are truly the centre of our world!' We were able to buy land in the foothills at Reinoso del Cerrato next to Villaviudas, my father's birthplace. We re-forested it with almond and other trees and named it Montepaz (Peace Hill). From our land, we can see, down the hill, Villaviudas cemetery where my parents are buried. Montepaz is where I meditate and write about the future of humankind and nature.

Ikeda: What you say conjures up beautiful images of Spain. Bathed in the strong sunlight of southern Europe, yours is truly a land of passion and cheerful people strong enough to overcome all obstacles.

The passionate people of the Spanish Canary Islands also demonstrate great solidarity and friendship. I remember warmly encouraging my associates there by saying 'Columbus moored at the Canary Islands on his way to discovering the New World. I hope the people of these islands will foster a new series of navigators to pioneer the age of humanism.'

Díez-Hochleitner: I have more chances to visit the southern part of Spain now than when I was young. Madrid has a pleasant climate: though it is hot there, you can always escape the heat by travelling to the nearby mountains. But for me, the most important element is the warmth of the human heart. The best place to live is the place where you find friendship and understanding. Furthermore, among many old and perhaps illiterate people, one is often blessed with the wisdom of their respective cultural identities.

Ikeda: I agree. Depression and friction in human relations spoil even the most attractive climate. Human beings also have the strength to make the most inhospitable environment a place for self-development. In his *A Geography of Human Life*, Tsunesaburo Makiguchi wrote, 'But it is through our spiritual interaction with the earth that the characteristics which we think of as truly human are ignited and nurtured within us. Our spiritual interactions with our surroundings are almost endless in variety and diversity.'[1] A natural setting rich in friendship, wisdom and trust inspires us with radiant hope.

Díez-Hochleitner: That is certainly true. Many visitors to Spain go to the Costa del Sol for the sun and the sea. I am not interested in sunbathing; however, present climate change trends and increasing global warming may mean that, before long, we may have to go to Northern Europe instead, for sunlight without excessive heat and dryness – let us hope that does not happen!

Ikeda: The weather has certainly been strange for the past few years. The heat wave that struck Europe in the first half of August 2003 caused immense damage. Many people died: more than 1,000 in Spain, more than 1,300 in Portugal and more than 10,000 in France. Opinions differ on whether the heat wave was connected with global warming, but whatever the relation, reducing the damage involves many different policies related to natural science, medical therapy and welfare.

Your own home town Bilbao is located in the Basque region, famous all over the world for natural beauty. What do you find especially attractive about it?

Díez-Hochleitner: Its gentle mountains are the most appealing part of the Basque Vizcaya province. A climb to the top is relatively easy, and from the narrow trails leading down, one can enjoy views of pine forests and grassy fields, the fragrances of which blend with the tangy sea air from the coast. Called the Estuary of

23

Bilbao, the River Nervión is both part of the sea and a tidal river, and is in fact the backbone of the city.

The region is a series of valleys, rolling hills and craggy mountains. When I was young, walking in the mountains strengthened me physically; indeed, it was my principal form of exercise. However, the best part was the friendships I made with the inhabitants, meeting them in their rural homes – *caserios* – surrounded by land grazed by cattle.

The city of Bilbao itself is both busy and elegant, particularly with the opening of the Guggenheim Museum and the ongoing urban renewal of its surroundings.

Ikeda: The Basque Autonomous Community (Communidad Autónoma del Páis Vasco) is one of the seventeen autonomous communities and two autonomous cities that form the Spanish kingdom. Each has its own rich cultural heritage, evolving harmoniously alongside the others. The concept of such accord sets a perfect example for all humanity.

Díez-Hochleitner: Yes, unity is the great gift Spain has gained from a long history and peaceful transition after dictatorship, thanks to the leadership of King Juan Carlos. Spain has experienced the Christian civilization of the West and the Islamic civilization of the East. As you say, within our country there are many different cultural traditions, all of which are connected by a strong bond. When asked about blood lineage, my wife always says, 'Like all Spaniards, I also have Arab and Jewish blood in my veins.' Upon hearing this, people often cannot conceal their surprise. But in addition to Arab and Jewish blood, Celtic, Gothic, Roman and Phoenician blood most probably flows in our veins too. My German grandmother's line comes from Switzerland (near Zurich), and her name, Hoeng, is said to be of Asian derivation. This is a wonderful thing – showing that the world is integrated and becomes more so every day.

Ikeda: With globalization, computer technology and advanced communications, the move towards uniting the world has become irreversible. We are at a turning point where greater inter-society

24

understanding through dialogue has become increasingly critical. Humanity can learn a great deal from Spain's history of harmony and fusion.

Díez-Hochleitner: It is good of you to say so. All peoples – Jews, Muslims, everyone – deserve respect. I much prefer to speak about profound *respect* rather than just *tolerance*. Although I am a European, many of my friends and colleagues are Israelis, Palestinians and people from the Arab, African, Asian and American nations.

Ikeda: Friendship binds people together and encourages global peace. That is why I have engaged in candid dialogues with individuals of different religious and philosophical backgrounds, including Arnold J. Toynbee, Aurelio Peccei, Majid Tehranian, Nur O. Yalman, Zhou Enlai, Mikhail S. Gorbachev and Nelson Mandela. The range of dialogues conducted by SGI covers all parts of the globe, including Europe, the United States, Asia, South America and Africa. Through mutual learning in relation to nationality, ethnicity, culture and art, we are seeking amity and common understanding. For the sake of those of us who are interested in Spain, let us continue our discussion of your homeland.

Díez-Hochleitner: I shall be delighted; I am very fond of talking about my beloved homeland. In any case, let me just say how much I admire your openness to all cultures and beliefs, shown in your writings and dialogues with a considerable variety of well-known and highly respected personalities, among them my dearest friend, the founder of the Club of Rome and my predecessor as its president.

Ikeda: Spain and Japan have engaged in exchanges for about four and a half centuries. St Francis Xavier (1506–52) was the first Spaniard to visit Japan. How do Spaniards today regard him? Which Japanese people are famous in Spain?

Díez-Hochleitner: Francis Xavier is probably more famous in Japan than in Spain, although he is highly regarded as a missionary. I am at a loss for an answer to your question about Japanese people who are famous in Spain, besides the basic knowledge about your emperors and leading politicians. Famous Japanese names are those of high-tech and reputed industrial brands. The Spanish regard the Japanese as highly capable, intelligent and cultivated. But I cannot call up names of specific individuals that are really famous nowadays in Spain. For me personally, of course, the Japanese person most deserving of respect is Daisaku Ikeda!

Ikeda: You are too kind. But putting myself aside, Japanese people tend to operate in groups of faceless individuals, due to their frustrating insularity and ineptness in social contexts.

To return to the Spanish, how do you account for the appeal of bullfighting and flamenco?

Díez-Hochleitner: I must say at the outset that I am no fan of bullfighting, an activity that many of my foreign friends find atrocious. But the Spanish do not go to bullfights because they love blood and death. Indeed they strongly disapprove of repeated or inept thrusts at the bull. I think the Spanish attend bullfights as an art form, a ballet of life and death between the bull and the bullfighter.

Ikeda: I see. And what about flamenco?

Díez-Hochleitner: My contact with flamenco started mainly thanks to my travelling to Andalusia in southern Spain. The open-natured Andalusians take joy in everything. They sing frequently and join their children in fun-loving festivals. I developed an affinity with them and began to understand that flamenco dance and music are a product of the culture that gushes forth from the Andalusian heart. Instead of the tourist attraction I had once taken it to be, it is something the Andalusians feel deeply about. Flamenco is a style – not the only one – of artistic expression representative of Spain. Music and peace go hand in hand. In the African Masai language the words for music and peace are the same!

Ikeda: Art expressing the energy of life has great power to move the human mind. The writings of Nichiren contain the following passage: 'Even if you are not Shariputra, you should leap up and dance. When Bodhisattva Superior Practices emerged from the earth, did he not emerge dancing? And when Bodhisattva Universal Worthy arrived, the ground shook in six different ways.'[2] That is to say, art, including dancing, is a sublimation of miraculous human life, promoting mutual understanding and universal communication.

Now turning to the topic of painting, why was Spain able to produce such twentieth-century masters as Pablo Picasso, Joan Miró and Salvador Dali?

Díez-Hochleitner: I believe it was because of the light in Spain, which produces shadows that cast forms in sharp relief. Mediterranean sunlight acts like a lubricant for an art manifesting the very spirit of beauty. There is such a thing as specifically Mediterranean creativity: Sorolla being another outstanding example. But central Spain has also produced such well-known masters as Goya, Velázquez, Greco and Murillo, not to mention current hyper-realists.

Ikeda: Undeniably, the powerful sunlight of the Mediterranean produces pronounced contrasts of light and shade and clarifies outlines.

Díez-Hochleitner: One must turn to Japan for talent in high-tech organizational abilities. To learn of teamwork, one must go to the United States. The Spanish, however, can teach about local colour and the diversity of local populations, sunlight, richness of expression in communication, uproarious laughter, astonishing garrulity and, above all, creative imagination. I believe these are the things that enabled Spain to produce artistic masters and, I hope, will do so in the years to come.

Ikeda: In addition to bullfighting, flamenco and painting, Spain has a distinctive literary culture. Cervantes's *Don Quixote* has been translated into more than sixty languages and is read the world over. In my youth, it was one of my favourite books. Dostoevsky said it would be impossible to find anything deeper and more powerful anywhere in the world and called it the greatest and the final word on human thought.

Díez-Hochleitner: The book is, above all, the most outstanding treasure and reference of our language. It reflects, furthermore, a human image the Spanish would like to emulate, even though they know that in reality they do not. The ideal of most Spaniards – as well as of most people around the world, I hope – is the boldly speaking, magnanimous, serious person who preserves high values, broad ideals and protects the destitute. Thus Don Quixote is an attractive model for everyone. Nonetheless, although most would wish to become a chivalrous, gentlemanly leader like the Don Quijote de la Mancha, they also want to live simply and peacefully like his faithful, pot-bellied, clever servant Sancho Panza.

Ikeda: At one point in the novel, Don Quixote says, '(A person) must . . . be valiant in his deeds, patient in his afflictions, charitable towards the needy and, in fact, a maintainer of truth, although its defence may cost him his life.'[3] The light of Cervantes's truth shines bright down the ages.

Another great Spanish literary figure is the poet Federico García Lorca (1898–1936). His poem 'Little Ballad of Three Rivers' contains this passage:

> Ah, love, that fled
> and never returned!
> Bear orange blossoms, Andalucia,
> and olives to your seas.
> Ah, love, that fled
> through the air!

Díez-Hochleitner: I see that you are very familiar with his work.

Ikeda: Thank you for saying so. García Lorca was shot during an internal uprising in Spain (the 1936–9 Spanish Civil War) when he was only 38 years old. His short but passionate life made a profound impression on me.

Díez-Hochleitner: I am also very fond of García Lorca's work. Antonio Machado (1875–1939) from Castile is another poet who impresses me, perhaps because, although having been born and raised in Bilbao, I too trace my roots to Castile. He argued that human acts are not the fruit of a moment of conscience and passion but are the result of a whole lifetime's actions, and constitute the essence of the individual.

High-quality life-long education and learning for all (humanism and training), contributing to sustainable development and peace around the world, have increasingly become the goals I strive for and the raison d'être throughout my life. My Spanish roots – based on a culture always wide-open to the world – have helped me become, and feel like, a real world citizen, always deeply involved with international organizations and activities.

Ikeda: From my mentor Josei Toda, I inherited the clear goal of world peace; throughout my whole life, I have striven to achieve it. Some of the things SGI and I have done include the exhibition 'Nuclear Weapons: Threat to Our World',[4] held at the United Nations Headquarters in New York; promotion of peace movements in various parts of the world; and peace proposals made annually since 1983. I also strive to create a network of peace from the perspective of human rights and the environment. I intend to continue this kind of work for the rest of my life.

In this short discussion, I think we have shown that, in addition to its long history and rich cultural heritage, Spain is a land of interpersonal exchange, good cheer and a vibrant, humane, communal spirit.

FOUR

King of Spain

Ikeda: On 11 February 1998, a group of leaders from various fields gathered at the Manila Hotel for a gala ceremony to confer the Knight Grand Cross of Rizal on His Majesty Juan Carlos I, King of Spain. My wife and I were visiting the Philippines at the time and received an invitation to attend. As I had been the first recipient of the order, they asked me to join the celebration. I had the honour of handing the certificate to the king before a group of a thousand people, and he shook my hand with a smile.

I dedicated a long poem to him entitled 'Al Gran Rey de la Paz, Sol de España', (To the great king of peace, the sun of Spain) which praised the way he had led his country to democracy. I had already met him in a separate room before the ceremony and became aware of his strong personality and elegance.

Díez-Hochleitner: I was delighted to hear of your meeting with the king, who commented favourably on it.

Ikeda: I am deeply honoured. It is always darkest just before the dawn; like the rising sun, King Juan Carlos brought a new dawn to Spain. For thirty-six years until it ended in 1975, the Franco regime violated human rights and isolated Spain from the rest of Europe.

1. Daisaku Ikeda congratulates their Majesties King Juan Carlos and Queen Sofia of Spain on their receiving the Knight Grand Cross of Rizal

On a visit in 1961, I found Madrid surprisingly deserted and sad; on the surface, peace and order prevailed, but I sensed desperation and suffering among the people, due to the underlying lack of freedom.

Twenty-two years later, in 1983, Madrid had become a totally different, very lively place. With the fastest-growing economy in Europe, the country successfully hosted the Barcelona Olympics and the World Exposition in Seville in 1992. King Juan Carlos was the nucleus of that great transformation. But before discussing him further, I should like to ask you about Francisco Franco (1892–1975), who defeated the forces of the republic and set up a dictatorship in 1939.

Díez-Hochleitner: Franco's potential, which might have served Spain, failed it totally. In his youth he was among the youngest, most brilliant Spanish officers in Morocco, a Spanish protectorate at the time. As far as I know, he was not among the initial plotters before the outbreak of the Spanish Civil War. However, the military soon chose him to command the fighting.

The full truth is unknown, but after the deaths of the leading fascists and nationalists who planned to rebel against the republic, Franco seized power himself. Suddenly the general who had been employed to command the military revealed an ambition for absolute power.

Ikeda: And oppression set in?

Díez-Hochleitner: The republican forces were defeated by Franco's military strategy and barbaric, oppressive acts. Of course, any war is horrendous, but the killing on both sides of a million Spaniards was extraordinarily horrendous. Most deplorable, however, was the retribution carried out on the republican forces after Franco's victory. Many republicans were shot on the basis of hasty, summary sentences.

In the years after the Civil War, Spain entered a period of darkness. The Second World War was followed by a time of economic hardship and widespread famine. Deprived of all rights and incapable of political action, the people were compelled to simply submit and accept their position.

Ikeda: How did such a regime manage to survive for thirty-six years?

Díez-Hochleitner: The Franco regime oppressed the people; in conditions of domestic poverty, hatred and jealousy thrived. When the economy took a turn for the better and living standards improved, the people began demanding democracy. Living under a dictatorship, they found actual resistance hard to imagine; there were not many heroes in a world of silence and submission. When the Cold War started, the West – particularly the USA – formed ties with the Franco regime in its search for anti-Communist allies.

Ikeda: Long oppression under a dictatorship freezes people's minds. Having no hope of being able to change things makes them feel impotent. From the age of 10, Prince Juan Carlos lived in Spain under Franco's domination; forced into a position of subordination, he waited for his chance to ascend the throne.

He was determined to promote democratization; violent revolution was out of the question. It would evoke opposition from the old system, thus increasing the danger of another civil war and anarchy. However, when he became king, Juan Carlos's brilliant leadership avoided this situation. He reintegrated his formerly estranged nation back into Europe and the world, without bloodshed.

Most startling of all was the king's action during the situation. He was believed to be an incompetent, pliant puppet, but actually he was only biding his time: when he ascended the throne, he was seen to be a courageous, imposing and outgoing individual. Using his abilities to avoid schism, he brought about reform peacefully; while building on the old system, he introduced fresh blood by surrounding himself with outstanding younger people. Three years later, he had converted a rigidly totalitarian state into a democratic parliamentary monarchy, based on the British model. How did you react to these changes in the king?

Díez-Hochleitner: Personally I was not surprised at all. The words and deeds that amazed the Spanish people after he ascended the throne were present in him from his early days as crown prince. I first met him when I was an international civil servant at the Organization of American States (OAS), World Bank, UNESCO and so on. Appointed number two within the Spanish Ministry of Education and Science in 1968, with Juan Carlos's backing, I frequently met the crown prince, who wished to be regularly and fully briefed on Spanish educational reform. To him, equal educational opportunities and development were and are a *sine qua non* in enhancing democracy.

In January 1971, President Richard Nixon invited him to Washington, Juan Carlos's first state-sponsored overseas visit as crown prince. He chose me to accompany him as his civil attaché. On our way to Washington, he made a brilliant thirty-minute speech – without a written text – in flawless English to hundreds of officers and students at the Naval Academy in Annapolis.

In closed-door discussions with leading people in Washington, he broached extremely important topics. He mentioned his desire to be a king who was faithful to Spain, who would contribute to the nation and who would be the monarch of the whole Spanish people. He also expressed his hope that Spain would rejoin the world and become a constitutional monarchy capable of making contributions to democracy.

Before his accession to the throne, he was thought to have no opinions of his own. This reputation was the result of a careful strategy; prime ministers Carrero Blanco and Arias Navarro, who had been true to the dictatorship, believed they could remain in power after Franco's death as long as the king willingly took orders from them and did his utmost for the continuity of the Franco system. Their expectations were very wide of the mark.

This is why my own opinions of King Juan Carlos have not altered from the outset. Convinced that he was already a proponent of democracy long before he became crown prince, I understood his actions.

Ikeda: In these times, when evil breeds evil and violence breeds violence, people in high places can learn much from the enlightened leadership of the King of Spain.

Díez-Hochleitner: I have worked for years on education and development planning, knowing full well that plans are seldom implemented in their original form, but I have seen a rare example of such implementation in the person of the king. Initially people thought success would be impossible because of hatred, struggle and schism. Nonetheless, we made it through the pre-transition years; that is, the years before real transition to democracy. I strongly and openly respect the king, as he was responsible for this success.

Given the mediocre leadership currently evident around the world, people like our king are more necessary than ever. If I may say so, your messages and activities in your own fields are increasingly important and necessary today, as the world confronts crucial situations.

Ikeda: Your praise of me is too generous. Kant said that under all circumstances human beings must regard both themselves and others as ends, never as mere means; everything depends on whether we abide by his dictum. The same attitude is essential to good leadership as well.

The vital issue is how leaders relate to human beings. Is leadership founded on a belief in humanity? Does it connect human beings and develop their potential? Or, founded on distrust, does it foster schism, treat people as tools, and suppress their potentials? These are the factors that distinguish humanistic leadership from totalitarian leadership.

The noblest ideals and strategies will be obstructed unless their implementers assume the right view of humanity. That is why leadership must be based on trust in humanity. It all begins and ends with humanity: the confusion of current times arises from the deluded notion that, even if leaders lack common humanity, things will come out all right as long as they create suitable concepts and structures. Solving difficult problems demands great leadership.

Díez-Hochleitner: I agree completely. The King of Spain is a man of great integrity; his solid leadership abilities, perspicacity, sensitivity, flawless, coherent behaviour and his extraordinary humanity have always deeply impressed me. Such qualities explain why he is king of the entire Spanish people. On the basis of your views on leadership, we can build a renewed, solid base for prompt, new, face-to-face East–West encounters. Both humanity and nature are greatly in need of them.

Ikeda: King Juan Carlos has united the sundered, changed despair into hope, converted dictatorship into democracy and made the impossible possible. From the age of 10 he faced many difficulties, but, on the basis of this experience, he built within himself, in his heart, a pillar of profound trust in human beings. He is a living image of the humanistic leadership desperately needed in the twenty-first century.

We must avoid the clashes of civilizations that some people talk about. To do so, leaders must steadfastly insist on dialogue as the prime means of problem resolution. I greatly admire your remarks about the necessity of East–West exchanges. SGI remains consistently committed to fostering such exchanges.

FIVE

Global *Problematique*

Ikeda: The Club of Rome, of which you are honorary president, was one of the earliest organizations to issue warnings about the complex interdependence of worldwide problems, including global warming, atmospheric pollution, depletion of the ozone layer, acid rain, desertification and the destruction of forests.

Díez-Hochleitner: Yes. These issues, and pertinent population studies, were at the core of our early debates. At our first meeting, held at the Academy Lincei in Rome in 1968, the decision was taken to invite, through Professor Jay Forrester, a team of experts from the Massachusetts Institute of Technology to prepare a report on the current state and future prospects of these and any other global issues. As a result, in 1972, Dennis and Donella Meadows published *The Limits to Growth: A Report for the Club of Rome's Project on the Predicament of Mankind*.

Ikeda: The impact the report had on the world was on a scale rare in recent years. Its far-sightedness captured attention across the world and led me to undertake a dialogue on the global *problematique* with Aurelio Peccei, founder of the Club of Rome.

Díez-Hochleitner: Our previous talk about your meeting and dialogue with Dr Peccei made a profound impression on me. When I became president of the Club of Rome in 1990, we decided to bring the report up to date and expand it. Not least, we underlined the key role of love in its compassionate form in the search for valid and viable solutions.

Consequently, the report was reissued in 1992 under the title *Beyond the Limits: Confronting Global Collapse, Envisioning a Sustainable Future*. A third version has been published more recently, entitled: *The Limits to Growth: The 30-Year Update*.

Ikeda: The Japanese edition aroused great interest.

Díez-Hochleitner: Many other relevant global issues were discussed, including governance, ethical values, science and technology, and education above all. Education has always been my own main field of interest and professional activity, particularly in preparing the report published in 1979 as *No Limits to Learning: Bridging the Human Gap*. In *The Limits to Growth*, we warned of the destruction to which continuing population expansion and economic growth lead, mainly due to the imbalance in the distribution of the world's population vis-à-vis the region's capacity to support that population. In *Beyond the Limits*, we argued that humanity has already passed the stage at which growth can be continued without burdening the environment. At the same time, we indicated new developments that would make a solution to the problem possible. We stated that, in many instances, the speed with which human beings waste essential natural resources and emit pollutants has already exceeded physical sustainability. We then expressed our belief that there is still room for human wisdom and creativity if we immediately reflect on and correct our actions. This same approach has been followed in the recent third version, *The Limits to Growth.: The 30-Year Update*.

Ikeda: Now, several decades later, the points made in the first report remain pressing. Though the situation is difficult, it would be pointless simply to give up. The global environmental problem involves complicated elements; but, since human beings created them all, human beings can deal with them. Doing so requires consolidating international public opinion and cultivating popular solidarity.

Although time consuming, education is the foundation for all reforms. To the World Summit on Sustainable Development held in South Africa in August 2002, I proposed that we build a sustainable future through the power of broad-based education on protecting the environment. I also suggested that the Earth Charter be enthusiastically used as material for education on the environment in schools and elsewhere.

Saving the environment requires a global revolution that must start with individual human revolutions. That is the road to the solution of the complex of worldwide problems.

Díez-Hochleitner: It is indeed. With compassion and a sense of responsibility, we must prepare models for future lifestyles. Only the human revolution can develop our inherent strengths, fully enlighten us to our essential nature and enable us to act in accordance with it. The human revolution is the only way for us to use computers, satellites, machines, atomic generators and electronics wisely for the sake of our fellows, in ways that will work harmoniously with our terrestrial environment and even with the whole universe.

This kind of globalization, instead of egoistic, ignorant globalization serving only the interests of the richest and most powerful, is not only desirable, but also probably essential.

Ikeda: Yes, education is highly important. Humanity must be our starting point in it, as in everything.

Global warming, one of the steadily worsening environmental problems facing us today, is said to be caused, at least in part, by increased carbon dioxide emissions. Measurements of global carbon dioxide concentrations began at the South Pole in 1957. At that time, the mean was 315 parts per million (ppm). In 2003 the world average was 374ppm. In 2004, in the vicinity of Japan the figure was 380ppm. Statistics of increasing average global temperatures were first taken in 1880. Since then the average has grown by about 0.7 degrees Centigrade per century. The temperature for 2004 was the fifth highest, after 1998, 2002, 2003 and, last but not least, 2006. Another cause for concern is the decrease in the surface area covered by ocean ice, which in the winter of 2004 was the smallest it had been since 1979.

Díez-Hochleitner: Yes, and as well as global warming, the oceans are becoming seriously polluted. Although pollution of fresh water on land masses is frequently discussed, people seem to forget about seawater, although it accounts for most of all water on Earth.

A treasury of life forms, the oceans can absorb carbon dioxide, exchanging harmful gases for beneficial ones in amounts exceeding the oxygen–carbon dioxide exchange produced by our forests. Nonetheless, insufficient measures are being taken to protect them; petroleum films on the ocean surface destroy vast amounts of plankton, immense coral reefs are dying. Decisive steps to deal with petroleum pollution and global warming have yet to be taken.

Ikeda: As you imply, human actions directly influence the marine ecosystem on a global scale. One example is the way nitrogen and phosphorus from the land affect marine nutrition, causing the harmful algal blooms known as red tides. Recently, it has been discovered that these red tides occur when ordinary diatoms change into highly toxic dinoflagellates as a result of changes in the nitrogen–phosphorus balance in shore and estuary regions. Increases in phosphorus accompanied by decreases in nitrogen stimulate massive growths in dinoflagellate numbers. Dam construction is often cited as the cause of this phenomenon. In other words, human actions destroying nature's delicate balance make our living Earth - our Gaia - very sick indeed.

Díez-Hochleitner: This complicated issue is critical to the continued existence of humanity. Many environmental problems are the consequences of our irresponsibly ignorant behaviour or of our failure to rectify human actions that harm the planet. Disregarding moral and ethical controls, we go on doing things we ought not to do.

Ikeda: You go straight to the heart of the matter. In his *Believing Cassandra: An Optimist Looks at a Pessimist's World*, the journalist and environmental conservation activist Alan AtKisson describes the crisis in terms of 'delays in feedback'.

Díez-Hochleitner: Worsening pollution of the planet and the continuing imbalanced population explosion – with a rapidly growing proportion of urban-dwellers – creates a situation that brooks no delay. In a vicious circle, the population explosion and urban concentration worsen the environment, the worsened environment generates more poverty, which in turn leads the population to increase. In both of our reports, we of the Club of Rome said that Earth can no longer tolerate the present rate of economic growth based on consumerism and resources waste. We realize, however, that people in developing countries want to enjoy the prosperity enjoyed by the industrialized nations.

No improvement has been made in dealing with the poverty problem that we lamented decades ago; indeed, it has worsened and is now getting out of hand. In addition to being important on humanitarian grounds, eliminating poverty would contribute to peace and benefit the environment, too. Meanwhile, we are faced with the 'shame and scandal of poverty', which happens to be the title of another report to the Club of Rome.

Ikeda: Precisely. World leaders must pool their wisdom and devote all their energy to solving the poverty problem that is seriously disrupting the world order.

In one of my annual proposals on SGI Day in 2000, I suggested what might be called a global Marshall Plan for dealing with the poverty problem. Also, in addition to its work in the name of nuclear disarmament, the Toda Institute for Global Peace and Policy Research, which I founded, is now dealing with this poverty problem as a focal issue of our age. According to the UN Millennium Development Goals (9 June 2005),

> from 1990 to 2001, rates of extreme poverty fell rapidly in much of Asia – with the number of people living on less than $1 a day dropping by nearly a quarter of a billion people (from 936,000,000 to 706,000,000) but in sub-Saharan Africa, which already had the highest poverty rates in the world, millions more fell deep into poverty (from 227,000,000 to 313,000,000).

Díez-Hochleitner: The gap between rich and poor is a fundamental factor in the growth of violence and terrorism. That fact by no means justifies violence and terrorism, but we must realize that terrorists find recruiting easier among poverty-stricken people. To make the continued coexistence of Earth and humanity possible, we must discover a way to eliminate social injustice totally, and a way to preserve the environment.

Ikeda: Certainly the planet is in a pathological condition symptomized by the poverty and environmental problem, but the fundamental issue is the pathological condition of humanity itself. In *The Limits to Growth*, the Club of Rome asked how we can bequeath a livable global environment to posterity. The key point is 'livable-ness'. All people must have a fair share of the good life, and the environment must receive its share of attention too. Ensuring that these things happen is closely connected with the Club of Rome's concern for a sustainable future.

Díez-Hochleitner: I agree. For the benefit of future generations we must cure humanity's problems while preserving the capacity of our planet to support this.

Ikeda: The Buddhist doctrine known as *Esho-funi* in Japanese teaches that, though they appear as different phenomena, life (*sho*) and the environment (*e*) are essentially one indivisible whole.

In a wise, powerful statement, the great Japanese priest and philosopher Nichiren (1222–82) wrote, 'To illustrate, environment is like the shadow, and life, the body. Without the body, no shadow can exist, and without life no environment.'[1] In other words, environmental phenomena (*e*) cannot exist without human life (*sho*). The preservation and revival of the environment depend on our ability to evoke and develop wisdom from human life.

Díez-Hochleitner: Harmony with the environment can be seen as a symphony of nature and humanity. Thus, the Club of Rome can learn much from Buddhist teachings and the Soka Gakkai movement.

42

Ikeda: In *Believing Cassandra*, AtKisson wrote:

> The precise location of the problem that is driving the World to the brink of collapse, and pushing Nature dangerously out of balance, can be found at those critical points where the World and Nature are intimately communicating with each other. The problem is, they *aren't.* . . . The feedback signals coming back from Nature to the World – telling us that sources are falling, or sinks filling – arrive too slowly, or not at all, or get ignored on arrival.[2]

To lend an ear to warnings from nature, we must recognize our own relationship with the environment and base our actions and thoughts on principles such as the indivisibility of life and environment. ·

Díez-Hochleitner: I agree. In addition to pointing out things like global warming and ocean pollution as the causes of Earth's illness, we must engage in a sort of dialogue with Gaia. Humanity must return to the bosom of nature. Instead of talking about our rights in connection with nature, we must realize that we all share responsibility for it. We can learn much from Soka Gakkai as far as the relationship between life and environment is concerned.

Ikeda: In our dialogue *Before It Is Too Late*, Aurelio Peccei said,

> . . . the gamut of still dormant capacities available in each individual is so great that we can make of them the greatest human resource. It is by grooming and developing these capacities in a way consistent with our new condition in this changed world – and only in this way – that we can again put a modicum of order and harmony in our affairs, including our relations with Nature, and thus move safely ahead.[3]

Each human life is endowed with limitless potential for overcoming all difficulties and creating a new age of order and harmony. The question is how to develop that potential. This is the most fundamental issue of the twenty-first century.

Of course, to conserve the global environment, we must have concrete knowledge of the current situation and learn and implement policies and standards, but what is now needed most is for us to conquer our narrow egoism. For the sake of the happiness of both the self and others, each individual urgently requires a reliable, symbiotic philosophy and course of action. I am convinced that this is the key to successful conservation.

2. Copies, in several editions, of Before It Is Too Late, *co-authored by Aurelio Peccei and Daisaku Ikeda, published in sixteen languages*

SIX

Light and Shadow of Globalism

Díez-Hochleitner: In the preceding chapter, we discussed the report entitled *Beyond the Limits*, which was issued in 1992 as an updated report of the Club of Rome. Since then, the issue of globalization and interdependence has assumed great prominence, and has split world opinion. I regard globalization as an actual phenomenon that, while in itself neither good nor bad, can be put to good or bad use. Do you agree?

Ikeda: Yes. Transcending national boundaries in such fields as politics, economics and culture, globalization is influencing all humanity at an ever-faster pace. Transport and communication networks – symbols of the globalization process – are making new, richer interpersonal and intercultural relationships possible. Big businesses are no longer identified with specific countries. The Internet allows instant communication and information exchange with all parts of the globe; these new and fruitful encounters must be used to expand the network of mutual understanding, amity and peace.

Díez-Hochleitner: That is true. However, large-scale inter-cultural dialogues still have a long way to go.

Ikeda: The main problem today is that globalization is practically synonymous with Westernization. The result is that new encounters undoubtedly form a potential background for new collisions.

Díez-Hochleitner: Yes – humanity must be dealt with as a whole. The terrorist attacks on the United States on 11 September 2001 symbolize the situation: a lack of understanding between peoples who, although broadly similar, have different cultures and backgrounds. To understand the causes of the attacks and the nature of subsequent events, we must examine what preceded them; specifically, American actions up to that event.

I have great respect for the United States and its democracy: I worked for President Kennedy, my family and I have lived in the United States on two separate occasions, and therefore I feel I should be allowed to express my opinion.

For the sake of the America I know and love, and all the other people who love America, I cannot help being critical of the problems that the present hegemonic ambitions of America´s leaders pose for the world today.

Ikeda: Unfortunately, globalization tends to escalate regional conflicts into worldwide conflicts. The media constantly flash images of the dreadful spectacles of war to all parts of the planet. Psychologically unprepared people are confronted with examples of violence and hatred in far distant lands. The globalization of violence is on the rise – an example would be the train bombings in Spain on 11 March 2004, where over 200 precious lives were lost and more than 1,700 people were injured. I should like to take this opportunity to express my sincerest condolences to the victims.

Díez-Hochleitner: Allow me to thank you for the prompt telegram of condolence you sent me. Paradoxically, though I believe in human progress, at present we seem to be sliding back from peace to war. Conflicts are breaking out all over the world, although massacres that occur outside industrialized nations receive little interest or publicity.

Ikeda: The events of 11 September finally triggered interest in these areas of conflict, but the situation had been deteriorating for a long time before that.

Díez-Hochleitner: Yes, and in the real world terrorism is far more prevalent than the overt attacks. I am speaking of economic warfare waged by the industrialized nations: we strangle life, pollute our beloved planet and poison the human race, while creating intolerable economic disparities between the rich and poor.

Ikeda: That is true. One aspect of globalization is to expand a 'law of the jungle' economic struggle throughout the world; everywhere, the rich get richer and the poor get poorer.

Humankind seems to be facing one of those great historic changes, like the English Industrial Revolution or the French Revolution, that compel us to return to first principles. In his *The Theory of Moral Sentiments*, Adam Smith – best known for *The Wealth of Nations* – insisted that it is impossible to achieve efficiency without also aiming to be beneficent and humane. The single-minded quest for efficiency hinders humanity. Economic activities diverging from the human path give rise to economic conflict.

Díez-Hochleitner: Activities in the field of economics are simply tools for the development of a sustainable and humane society; otherwise, no economic theory is of any use. Inciting economic conflicts in the name of capturing markets impairs sustainable development.

Ikeda: The pursuit of humanity in this age of economic globalization imposes the urgent need to cultivate global citizens of great human sympathy.

In June 1994, I visited Glasgow University to receive an honorary doctorate – this was where Adam Smith studied and later taught. As well as his brilliant written work, he was a splendid teacher who emphasized the need for students' understanding above all else. In Smith's time, society was changing rapidly under

47

the influence of the Industrial Revolution, and I reflected on how Smith, seeing these alterations, devoted himself to education.

Díez-Hochleitner: As you imply, education is of the greatest importance. War does not simply involve killing – what about the injury done to people's minds? How often have we damaged other people's countries and cultures, fully aware that we were causing profound suffering, as we are doing to the Islamic world now?

The West owes a great deal to Islamic culture; the Renaissance, for example, would have been impossible without it. But today, due to the actions of a small percentage of extreme fundamentalists, any mention of Islam automatically evokes images of terrorists. Such an all-encompassing aggressive attitude is a kind of war – a war of the prejudiced spirit. Peace must develop from the pacifist mindset. World leaders must keep this in mind.

Ikeda: You make a very cogent point. The Lotus Sutra, the quintessential Buddhist scripture, teaches of the Five Impurities: impurity of desire, of thought, of living beings, of life span and of the age. The impurity of desire is the tendency to be ruled by the five delusive inclinations of greed, anger (aggressiveness), foolishness (egoism), arrogance and doubt. The impurity of thought refers to ideologies. Impurities of human beings rob us of creativity and debilitate us physically. Impurities of life span weaken the vital force and shorten life itself. When the impurities of human beings and life span are rampant, violence, prejudice and greed spread through communities, ethnic groups, nations and humanity as a whole. The impurity of the age refers to a condition in which an entire era is polluted. The five impurities have spread to many dimensions in the present epoch.

Díez-Hochleitner: Undeniably. Violence of all kinds – including the nuclear threat – is growing more apparent and is spreading to schools, homes and all corners of our society. While considering this trend, we should always keep in mind the list of five impurities set out in the Lotus Sutra. How can we halt the spread of violence and the phenomena associated with it? How can we win the struggle for peace without resorting to arms?

Ikeda: In the earlier dialogue of this series, you made a pertinent point when you identified the gap between rich and poor as a fundamental cause of violence and terrorism. In a 'survival of the fittest' society, the strong grow stronger and the voice of the weak goes unheeded. As the gap between rich and poor widens, it contributes to the creation of an unjust society. We must fundamentally change this negative structure; to do so, we need to have sympathetic, understanding discussions. That is why Aurelio Peccei said in our dialogue that we must heed and harmonize the ambitions of those who have plenty with the demands of those who are struggling desperately not to sink into devastating poverty.

Misunderstanding, prejudice, hatred and conflict generate the cycle of violence; refusal to engage in dialogue is related to this process. So the harder the situation, the more resolutely we must strive to promote dialogue. Our dialogues must heed the voices of the suffering; they must replace despair with hope. The leaders of international organizations, such as the United Nations, must promote dialogue of this kind and back it up with relevant action.

Díez-Hochleitner: For decades the United Nations has been promoting a culture of peace and forging ahead with peace education. I have been heavily involved in educational planning, reforms and research. Education is constantly expanding, progressing and improving. Nonetheless, in spite of all the teaching and discussions about peace, war is still tolerated. Why do we not resist it more resolutely?

Ikeda: As Dr Peccei said, violent acts and attitudes indicate pathological social and cultural conditions. We can return, though, to a society in which non-violent attitudes and approaches shed light on violence, exposing it as an aberration. Violence cannot change the world for the better – only non-violence can do that.

Having been part of the resistance during the Second World War, stubbornly resisting the brutal fascists, Dr Peccei renounced violence as the ultimate evil. His experiences made a profound impression on me. Arrested with some of his resistance comrades, he was subjected to cruel treatment; the fact that the violence highlighted the depravity of the tormentors, not of the tormented, impressed him profoundly. He was deeply moved by the spiritual strength of the victims: under the most extreme hardships they clung firmly to their ideals, no matter what the sacrifice. In this way, they showed him how noble and inviolable the human spirit can be, deepening his own absolute faith in humanity and the power of the human spirit.

Díez-Hochleitner: That is true. His philosophy and deeds were rooted in his war experiences. One of Dr Peccei's thoughts that I often remember was that not even imprisonment can take away our personal freedom and human dignity, provided that we remain free in our hearts and minds.

Ikeda: Globalization makes this an age of exchanges, some of which lead to conflict, but we must create a cultural environment in which people use non-violent dialogue to resolve those conflicts. As you point out, this is possible. Using violent means to resolve conflicts only globalizes violence.

Díez-Hochleitner: An important point. Certainly dialogue is indispensable if we are to get to know each other and promote mutual respect and eventually develop cooperation and friendship. Dialogue should not be an end in itself but seen as an indispensable first step towards solidarity and action.

Ikeda: Yes. We must tirelessly and persistently engage in dialogues based on education about peace and humane principles.

As you have said, it is crucial for peace that world leaders engage with a pacific mindset. Our friend Mikhail S. Gorbachev, who is apprehensive about the world situation following the 11 September attacks, told me that there is no point in remaining passive and inactive regarding lasting peace. We must ask ourselves how to deal with the problems and inconsistencies constantly arising in modern society. Whether we have war or peace depends on whether we choose to solve our problems with force or with dialogue.

I agree with him completely. Peace can only be built if we steadfastly choose dialogue to resolve the problems that continue to confront us.

Díez-Hochleitner: I agree. Mr Gorbachev – who is an honorary member of the Club of Rome – has the moral authority conferred by coherently practising what he preaches.

Ikeda: The Buddhist scriptures teach: 'All tremble at violence, all fear death. Putting oneself in the place of another, one should not kill nor cause another to kill' (*Dhammapada*, 129). Two points are especially important about this passage. First, it teaches us to transcend violence, greed and egoism by putting ourselves in other people's shoes and empathizing with their suffering. Second, it counsels helping others to transcend their violence and choose non-violence. Promoting the pacifist mindset in this way will spread its influence through society and all humanity.

Díez-Hochleitner: Sometimes we talk very casually about peace. What do we have in mind when we say 'peace'? Generally it is seen as the passive peace of a war-free situation, but to me that is not real peace. The chilling threat of nuclear weapons creates peace, but only in the sense of silence. True, during the Cold War, this fear played a part in averting numerous disasters; averting killing is good, but fear-induced peace is ridiculous. We must achieve an *active peace* involving dialogue, solidarity and cooperation.

Ikeda: Though it may provide temporary relief, trying to disrupt the cycle of violence and hatred with hard measures like armaments is only treating the symptoms and actually prolonging the malaise.

Though more time consuming, the only way to effect a fundamental cure is through dialogue and exchange at all levels in order to tap into innate human goodness – the pacifist mindset and the spiritual power of non-violence.

In a New Year greeting he kindly sent me, Mr Anwarul K. Chowdhury, UN Under-Secretary-General, wrote:

> In this context, if the message of the culture of peace and the values of tolerance, understanding and respect for diversity is inculcated in children from an early stage by their families, I believe that in the coming decades the world will experience a distinct change for the better in our conflict and violence ridden societies.

I understand that both your parents were sincere pacifists and that your mother's first name actually means peace.

Díez-Hochleitner: Yes, 'friede' means peace in German. Both my Spanish father and my German mother suffered considerably under the totalitarian regimes they encountered during the Spanish Civil War and the Second World War. Their inner peace, based on ethical and moral values, was enhanced by the consistency between their spoken convictions and their deeds. The example of my parents – always true to their peace-loving and democratic principles – has been a precious gift and guide throughout my life. I wish to bequeath this treasure to the families of my seven children and twenty-two grandchildren as the best inheritance I can offer.

Ikeda: A very moving wish. The road to true peace must begin with love for family and proceed to love for associates, friends, local communities, ethnic groups, nations and all humanity. In addition, it must include the desire for harmonious symbiosis with the world of nature. The all-important first step on this road is an education of peace principles. It takes courage to advance towards the great goal of peace: making it come true requires us to be as brave as Don Quixote was in the face of ridicule and revilement. Though the practically minded may laugh, we need quixotic courage to challenge everything in the fulfilment of such a great goal. I understand you are very fond of Cervantes's great book.

Díez-Hochleitner: Yes, indeed, it is the masterpiece of the Spanish language. As for Don Quixote, I especially like the part where he confronts the windmills he thinks are autocratic giants; that scene embodies real courage and idealism. A life without both ideals and action is meaningless.

Ikeda: Very true. The important thing is to cling to hope and ideals and never to give up. The difficulties of our time compel us to proclaim our courage and ideals boldly while moving forward towards the realization of the great goal of peace.

SEVEN

Globalization and World Citizenship

Ikeda: Please allow me to congratulate you on the expansion of the European Union and the birth of a greater unity involving some of the East European nations that were cut off from Western Europe during the Cold War. European unity is one of the great experiments of the twenty-first century; I wish it every success.

Count Richard Coudenhove-Kalergi – the father of European unity – and I shared several discussions that were published in Japanese in a collection called *Civilization, East and West*. Having witnessed the atrocities of the First World War, he dreamed of establishing lasting peace by creating a greater Europe. This recent development is surely a step towards realizing his vision.

Incidentally, I have spoken at length with André Malraux, who took part in the Spanish Civil War; he insisted that in the nuclear age humanity has no choice but to unify. As a hard-headed realist, though, he was pessimistic about the chances for peaceful union.

Díez-Hochleitner: With a Spanish father and a German mother (and a French daughter-in-law), I am delighted at the future prospect of the European Union and the hope it gives of a peaceful Europe. I welcome it all the more because I experienced at first hand the horrors of the Spanish Civil War of 1936–9 and, to a certain extent, through family members, the Second World War.

55

I am still uneasy, however, at the lack of a clear-cut European vision on the part of most Europeans, including, unfortunately, many politicians. In 1994, in Hanover, in my capacity as president, I convened the first annual Club of Rome conference, entitled 'Europe 2020'. The debates we held, in favour of an all-embracing Europe (from Brest to Vladivostok) to serve the world as an honest partner, not a new hegemonic power, still deserve to be read.

Ikeda: You have put your finger on a very important point, about which I hope we will have much more to say.

Díez-Hochleitner: Long before Jean Monnet's conception of the European Community, the great French writer Victor Hugo pioneered an extraordinary vision of the way Europe should be. For some articles that I was writing for publication in the Spanish press about that vision, I required documentary reference material, most of which I discovered in the magnificent collection you have

3. Victor Hugo House of Literature in Bièvres, founded by Daisaku Ikeda in 1991.

put together in your Victor Hugo House of Literature in Bièvres, near Paris.

Ikeda: I am glad the collection was of service to you. The spirit of Victor Hugo, the great humanist, becomes more radiant as the years pass. His profound observations and vision of the future are still of the greatest importance today. I should like to take this opportunity to say again how pleased and honoured I was that you took time from your busy schedule to attend the opening ceremony for our Victor Hugo House of Literature.

Towards the end of our set of dialogues, Aurelio Peccei discussed globalized society; he remarked that now, for the first time in history, all peoples and nations must consciously share the limited habitable environment of our planet. He said emphatically that our globalized society has but one destiny. Ultimately the fate of each individual is the same as that of the whole planet. This means that we must face a destiny shaped by the network of plans we ourselves have made for the use and protection of the environment, as it exists now.

As the Club of Rome perceived, environmental degradation is a planet-wide problem, which, like population, poverty and all the other issues confronting us, requires solutions on a global scale. Arriving at them is *our* job, because humankind shares a common, global destiny. Obviously, the expansion of the European Union is part of the progression towards these solutions.

Our age of globalized destiny needs world citizens now who are ready to work for the benefit of all humanity, because every one of us must think and act globally. As everyone knows, you are such a world citizen.

Díez-Hochleitner: Your opinion does me great honour. We all must feel and behave as world citizens and, to achieve this, we must examine our own roots. We are an important part of our complex planet and have a definite role to play. 'Think locally and act globally', together with 'think globally and act locally', are good recommendations to follow in this global world. Respect for inherited cultural diversity and sustainable global development are also solid guidelines for our role in life.

Ikeda: A blinkered society is governed by criteria conceived through narrow-mindedness. Human beings need a broad viewpoint and the strength to act.

Díez-Hochleitner: Actually, I once experienced a turning point that greatly broadened my outlook. It happened when I visited Tanzania as a member of a group of educational advisers during the presidency of Julius Nyerere, the father of Tanzanian independence. The only European in the group, I asked myself what I was doing there, as I had no affinity with the country. In fact, I looked down on the national culture, but the people turned out to be genuinely both kind and justly critical. In other words, they were so essentially human that finally I felt no distinction between them and people with whom I had always associated; I was able to perceive the inner persons behind their skin, faces and gestures. On the day of my departure, I told President Nyerere that I had undergone a change of heart and that the only major difference between us was the superficial one of skin colour.

Taking advantage of the opportunity he afforded me, I made a speech in which I told my audience how alien I had thought them at first, but that later I came to feel like one of them. I had discovered their beauty and had come to love them; I had made contact with Tanzania. Unbelievably, people began embracing me and the president proposed making me an honorary citizen. Had I never gone to Tanzania, I would never have had such a change of heart.

Ikeda: That is a wonderful story of an individual's human revolution.

Díez-Hochleitner: Humanity must be the focus of our attention, and self-examination must be our starting point. People who know their own capabilities can relate to others in a caring way. They can exert a truly humane influence by observing politics and by demanding that their leaders introduce reforms that prioritize the most pressing claims.

Ikeda: Precisely – everything must begin at home. If you want a well, start digging there and then. Great power is innate in a single human being; the important thing is to take the first step.

Díez-Hochleitner: You are correct in saying that dialogue can refresh and revive the planet. The unification of the globe will not diminish our diversity. Citizens of the world remain citizens of the world, no matter where they come from, but we must all begin at home by examining our roots because, if we know ourselves, we are more capable of knowing and understanding others.

Ikeda: The first president of Soka Gakkai, Tsunesaburo Makiguchi, who died while imprisoned for his struggle against militarism, insisted that each individual is simultaneously a citizen of their home region, of their nation, and of the world. Although our roots are at home, we still belong to our nation, and the stage on which we live out our lives is the world. Keeping the influences of home in mind enables us to become world citizens without being overpowered by national interests. You and Mr Makiguchi agree on this. A century ago, he prophesied that ultimately the era of military, political and economic competition will give way to one of humane competition, an environment for developing capable human beings. Education should play the major role for such development.

Considering it to be the most important factor, I have earnestly devoted myself to education, of which humanism and global citizenship are major ingredients. Internationalizing is the main focus of educating global citizens, which is why leaders from all over the world visit Soka campuses. Our student bodies are cosmopolitan: thirty-two countries and regions are represented at the Soka University of America, and twenty-one at the Soka University in Japan. Our aim is to use education to develop global citizens who consider the whole planet their home town.

Díez-Hochleitner: This illustrates your sweeping vision of education. As you know, education policies and reforms have been and continue to be the main concern of my whole professional life.

Cross-cultural education is fortunately becoming as indispensable as inter-disciplinary education.

Ikeda: In our dialogue, Count Coudenhove-Kalergi predicted the end of the East–West conflict and the intensification of the North–South conflict. The prophecy is coming true. As its title indicates, our dialogue dealt with East and West. Now dialogue must be expanded to include the North and the South – the whole global scene. With the hope of promoting this, I published a dialogue with the Iranian peace scholar Majid Tehranian. With its rich culture and history of contacts and fusion with the Islamic sphere, your homeland holds a key to the peace of the world.

Díez-Hochleitner: Yes, Spain can contribute to the North–South dialogue in many areas. We owe a great deal to Latin America. The Spanish conquered parts of South and Central America, from where they derived immense riches. Those people inherited Spanish culture and have become cultural brothers – we have learned and are still learning much from them. We also owe a debt to those that invaded Spain: the Arabs, for example, left us an important cultural heritage, and we should regard most, if not all of the Arab peoples as brothers. With this historical background, Spain is able to form respectful relationships with Latin-American and Islamic nations. As he has devoted himself to intercultural and inter-religious dialogue, I recommended to the Club of Rome that Prince El Hassan bin Talal of Jordan should succeed me as president. He was duly elected into the role. I hope that you and he will get to know each other well, even though he is no longer president.

Ikeda: That is very kind of you. Although I have not yet met him in person, I have had the honour of corresponding with the prince, and I was very pleased to receive an especially courteous letter from him.

I should like to take this opportunity to repeat my gratitude for his kind proposal to hold exhibitions at the annual general meeting of the Club of Rome. His idea was realized in the form of the 'Gandhi, King, Ikeda Exhibition', which is being promoted by Morehouse College in the United States, and the exhibition entitled 'Building a Culture of Peace for the Children of the World', produced by SGI in America (SGI-USA) and held in October 2003. On that occasion, Prince Hassan delivered a commemorative speech to a gathering of international intellectuals, in which he called on us to break with narrow nationalism, racism and discrimination and to build an international order and human solidarity founded on humanism and respect for human rights. He added that Mahatma Gandhi, Martin Luther King, Jr, and I have pointed the way to the path of mutual understanding and cooperation that humanity must follow.

Setting aside his kind words about me, his remarks clearly describe the world citizen who must fight against narrow nationalism, racism and discrimination. World citizens must strive to create human solidarity through non-violence and dialogue. Moreover, as you say, they must start here and now.

EIGHT

The Tripolar World:
The United States, Europe and Asia

Díez-Hochleitner: I should like to congratulate you on receiving an honorary doctorate from the University of Jordan on 22 July 2004. In his congratulatory letter to you, the Jordanian prince El Hassan bin Talal wrote, 'As a scholar and a religious man gifted with great comprehension and compassion, you have called us to higher thought and more thoughtful action.' His words express the respect that I too feel for you.

Ikeda: You are very kind to say so. Your words do me the greatest possible honour and inspire me to renew my determination to strive for world peace. In this context, our discussions of various aspects of the future of the world have great significance.

Díez-Hochleitner: I think so, too. Considerations of the future of the world involve a tripolar framework consisting of the United States, Europe and Asia. Instead of opposing one another, these three must contribute to worldwide, sustainable development through constructive mutual support and cooperation.

Ikeda: That is true. As all serious-thinking people agree, the time has come to call for a halt to confrontation. From the standpoint of human security, the structural violence caused by globalization – poverty, epidemics, environmental destruction and so on – grows distressingly grave.

As you stress, such structural violence and the social injustice of globalization are hotbeds for the growth of direct violence, like terrorism or internal warfare. Consequently, to eliminate anxiety about terrorism, the United States, Europe and Asia – world leaders in the political, economic and other spheres – must work together to build a fair and sustainable global community. Trends within the United States, now the sole superpower, are, of course, crucial.

Díez-Hochleitner: Whenever I have talked about the importance of dialogue and of strong leadership and value criteria, I have had the United States specifically in mind. Essentially, the United States can contribute constructively without using its might in destructive ways.

The future of the United States is of vital concern to all humanity because of its democratic values, its immense material success, and its obvious and great international influence. Unfortunately, however, as the sole current superpower, with its attitude of unilateral hegemony and rash leadership, the United States has made lamentable and grave mistakes both domestically and internationally.

Ikeda: Historically, military might has often failed to guarantee peace. In the world today, the number of issues that can be resolved militarily is limited. I greatly respect the way the United States has protected democracy and liberty and has contributed to world development. Today, though, the people of the world want the United States, as the sole superpower, to seek and pursue the goal of true peace for all humanity.

Díez-Hochleitner: In the past, immigration has made the United States a melting pot of the human race. Through social and economic development, the people of America have steadily striven to overcome all kinds of discrimination. On the other hand, Americans have also continually sought world leadership and hegemony. The character of the president – his vision, sincerity, capability – often greatly influenced the image and actions of the United States, but the special interests of big business can exert great pressure on a president, through lobbyists.

Ikeda: The military-industrial complex – pointed out by President Dwight D. Eisenhower and analysed by John Kenneth Galbraith – has a direct connection to the survival and happiness of the people of the world.

Díez-Hochleitner: The United States is always tempted to follow the path of military and economic hegemony. The course the nation pursues depends directly on the quality of the leaders of the time, and on the presence or absence of long-term pacific attitudes and international vision. Because of the danger of imperialistic ambitions and global conquest, the citizens of the whole world ought to be able to participate, in some way, in American presidential elections by making known their preferences. Field tests of this type of approach are already underway with the experimental electronic devices and network of the Global Referenda project. Were this to prove feasible, it might produce a degree of change.

Ikeda: The influence of the United States on the world is very great.

Díez-Hochleitner: Yes. Because I have been connected with it throughout my life, I have a very positive attitude towards the United States. My family and I lived in Washington DC, where I worked in several organizations: the Organization of American States, the Alliance for Progress and the World Bank. In addition, I have been a board member of foundations and scholarly organizations such as the International Council for Educational Development (ICED) and the Foundation for the Future (FFF), among others. Through this kind of work, I have come to understand, admire and love many aspects of the United States.

It would be an advantage for all humanity if the peoples of the world were able to help the Americans direct their positive attributes and progressive efforts. If we remain true to the spirit of multinational cooperation, we can build a peace-loving society that pursues justice, protects the environment and strives for sustainable development. True friends will criticize American deviations and mistakes, while striving to act in constructive ways to the advantage of humanity as a whole.

Ikeda: This is the role Europe has tried to play. What future role do you foresee for the North Atlantic Treaty Organization (NATO)?

Díez-Hochleitner: Although it is no doubt a useful international defensive tool, NATO needs to become more effectively linked to the UN system. Working openly together to bring peace to Iraq is essential if relations between the United States and Europe are to be stronger and more amicable in the years to come. At the same time, the aid to many other nations mediated by the United Nations is essential. To achieve global cooperation and peace, international law is of primary importance.

Ikeda: Although it may not be the ideal system for multinational cooperation, the world is certainly better off with the United Nations than it would be without it. We have no options other than enhancing, reforming and strengthening the United Nations, as it is essential to a world founded on international law. I share your opinion on this point, and make proposals to the United Nations on world betterment each year.

The United Nations came into being after the tremendous loss of life in the two world wars, after previous failed attempts like the Hague Peace Conferences and the League of Nations. Its primary goal is succinctly expressed in Article 1 of the preamble to its charter: 'To save succeeding generations from the scourge of war, which twice in our lifetime has brought untold sorrow to mankind. . .'. In other words, an assembly of humanity like the United Nations would not have come into being without that untold sorrow. The United Nations and the individual efforts of world citizens in the name of peace constitute a major historical force that should not be underestimated.

Díez-Hochleitner: Although I see no need for a world government, I do think world organizations like the United Nations, in which sovereign representatives of all member nations participate, are necessary. During wartime, representatives of those parties in conflict may temporarily withdraw.

Nations may entrust the resolution of various matters to the United Nations, by means of its own Parliament, without abdicating their sovereignty. In this sense, the United Nations is a place for conferring among governments, enterprises, foundations and non-governmental organizations (NGOs). Instead of making light of it, or avoiding providing ethical guidance in security-related issues, the United States ought to strive for the expansion and reform of important international organizations and should assume leadership in encouraging all nation states to join them.

Ikeda: Although some people argue that the Iraq war exposed the impotence of the United Nations, I disagree and feel that it proved its importance. Ironically, the troubles the United States encountered in Iraq demonstrate how important the multinational structure of the United Nations and the legitimacy it conveys are. Modern warfare involves general mobilization of the people, and each of the warring parties insists on the justice of its cause; sadly, you and I both know from historical experience how nation states kill in the name of justice. Since justice is often in the eye of the beholder, international law, which operates within a multinational framework, is our most rational recourse.

In his *Republic*, Plato said that 'justice' benefits the strong; it is now time to put an end to this millennia-old idea that might equals right. The most rational way to do so is to work out a multinational system of international law.

'Old' Europe, which in the twentieth century suffered the horrors of two major wars, set up a union or an alliance of the European nations in the search for multinational cooperation and peace; this experience carries great historical weight.

I believe that the issue of immigration will determine whether the great European experiment results in a model for a peaceful, prosperous world or in blocs of rich nations. Even France and the Netherlands, formerly tolerant towards immigrants, are apparently altering their policies.

Díez-Hochleitner: The nations of the European Union are trying to adjust laws on immigration between each other; at present internal boundaries are open among member nations. Ideally they should be open to peoples everywhere: this would truly make everybody a world citizen. However, the actual process is difficult and beset with obstacles; close cooperation with the immigrants' countries of origin is essential.

Ikeda: In her book *Losing Control? Sovereignty in an Age of Globalization*, the American sociologist Saskia Sassen said that whereas globalization is economic denationalization, immigrants renationalize governments. It is imprecise to say that globalization spells the decline of the state: even as globalization takes place, some governmental functions like border control and the security against terrorism and crime actually intensify. This tendency has become increasingly pronounced since 11 September. While cross-border movements from North to North or from North to South are free, movement from South to North is tightly restricted.

Díez-Hochleitner: Regional egoism must be overcome if all omni-directional migration is to be accepted. Open-door immigration policies frequently encounter opposition: lack of cooperation and cultural rejection hinder acceptance on the receiving side. Preventing this requires the creation of amicable relations in which local regulations are respected and institutions honoured within a framework of human rights.

What role do you envision for Japan in this context? You yourself contribute far more to the world than you learn from it. Indeed, your replies to my questions and your hopes in themselves constitute a contribution to the world. For decades, Japan has taken the lead in economic and technological development and has now established a strong position in the East. Like Germany in the period following the Second World War, Japan set the world a splendid example by restoring its sophisticated cultural and peace-loving traditions, and I believe that the teachings and practice of Soka Gakkai played a great role in this process.

Ikeda: Thank you for your kind words of understanding; I will leave objective evaluations of the role Soka Gakkai played in the postwar society of Japan to professionals. Suffice it only to comment that, during the postwar era of unconstructive ideological conflict, Soka Gakkai certainly did propagate the philosophy of peace among the ordinary people, thus creating a strong pacifist force in Japanese society.

Regarding what Japan should do: first, I believe that, with its praiseworthy Peace Constitution, it should lead the world by becoming a great pacifist and humane nation. Second, Japan must become a member of the Asian community in the truest sense; failure to form friendly ties with Asia would limit our options.

I have long insisted that, in terms of latent historical, cultural and political strength, China and India will join the United States and Europe as pivotal powers in the world: their importance is sure to grow in the coming years. For our own sake and for the sake of Asia and the rest of the world, Japan must strengthen cooperation with China and India.

Díez-Hochleitner: Yes, I understand. In my view, no just, peaceful global order is conceivable without the United States and Europe participating fully on an equal footing with Japan, China and India. Of course, Latin America, Africa and the Arab states must also take part.

One of the largest countries in the world, China is experiencing amazing economic growth and, given the accomplishment of promising, essential reforms, is sure to become a major world partner; everyone recognizes the need for it to do so. Thousands of years of cultural achievements are being revisited and giving China the attention it deserves; furthermore, Chinese society is going to be economically powerful both at home and among other Asian nations.

Ikeda: Japan rose to prominence in East Asia just over a hundred years ago; for thousands of years before that, Chinese civilization was the heart of Asia. In the early stage of its prominence, Japan overran China, although the Chinese people had never invaded Japan. Indeed historically, with a few exceptions, Chinese dynasties had never adopted aggressive attitudes towards neighbouring countries. In the light of this, it is nonsensical to exaggerate the Chinese threat.

I advocated normalizing Sino-Japanese relations as early as 1968. At the time, the Cultural Revolution made people talk of the Chinese threat even more than they do today. Nonetheless, I was adamant in insisting on normalization and the conclusion of amicable relations for the sake of future generations.

As the world changes at a dizzying pace, an East Asian community has already started to form. There can be no doubt that accelerating its formation will benefit Japan, Asia and the world.

Díez-Hochleitner: In the past few years, in addition to its great achievements in social and economical growth and democratization, India has been making extraordinary progress in higher education, science and cutting-edge technology. At present, Indian economic growth is astonishing. At the same time, like China, it has great wealth and valuable cultural diversity; I hope that India will continue providing the kind of spiritual inspiration it has provided in the past.

Ikeda: We Buddhists feel special respect for India – the spiritual superpower – as the birthplace of our religion. In more recent times, India has produced Gandhi, who illuminated the world with his philosophy of non-violence. In the political sphere, India was the leader of the non-aligned nations and continues to provide alternate viewpoints in international society.

Although recently overshadowed by international terrorism, the issue of global symbiosis dealt with in the Club of Rome's report *The Limits to Growth* is certain to become a central theme of international society once again. When that happens, the voice of India will be heeded even more for views on civilization, humanity and nature that are different from those espoused by modern Western culture.

Díez-Hochleitner: Fulfilling my duties as a representative of private groups or as an envoy of international and inter-government organizations, I have visited China and India on several occasions. That is why I have various reasons for respecting and lauding both countries. We must never forget that the total population of both countries is about half that of Earth as a whole. Like the rest of the world, Japan, China and India must overcome past animosities and work together for peaceful resolutions to issues. They must form close bonds of mutual cooperation; individually and together, these three countries can create a basis for world hope. In addition, the West must address the East face-to-face on an equal footing.

Ikeda: Exactly. We must avoid so-called clashes of civilizations: humanity living on an ailing Earth can no longer afford to engage in imperialism or power games. You from the West and I from the East must never stop urging the leaders of the world to engage in dialogue and cooperate in the name of harmonious coexistence.

NINE

Global Governance and a Revolution in Leadership

Díez-Hochleitner: Today's world leaders too often speak and act inconsistently, which is not the kind of leadership we need. What we need is impartial leadership that respects the environment and encourages cooperation among all ethnic groups to ensure the continued harmonious existence of the human race. The Earth is fundamentally ill, and the situation is getting worse; more serious than the physical crises, however, is the deep crisis in values and the growing scarcity of trustworthy leaders. We of the Club of Rome devote our best efforts to finding ways out of this dilemma. One contribution in this direction has been the report on *The Capacity to Govern*, which details the qualities and the training required.

Ikeda: In the admonitory report *The Limits to Growth*, published more than thirty years ago, the Club of Rome informed the world that material civilization had reached its limitations. We know what must be done but lack the decisiveness to do it; at the heart of this failure is the dearth of responsible leaders capable of seeing the whole picture. Too many nations are willing to ignore the plight of poor countries for the sake of increasing their own wealth; wrapped up entirely in the present, they ignore the fate of the children of the future.

Díez-Hochleitner: A world in which the satisfied and well-fed pay inadequate attention to others is gravely ill; such is the condition of our world today.

Ikeda: You once told me that the planet is sick because humanity is sick. Buddhism makes the basic observation that disorder in the environment and society always occurs because people's thoughts are troubled and unsettled.[1] Saving the planet requires changing the ideas and values propelling society; leaders' ethical, historical and social views directly affect the direction society takes.

The Club of Rome and Soka Gakkai International agree that only a human revolution – a change in our individual hearts and minds – can stimulate a revolution of the planet. We also must demand that world leaders undergo a human revolution; such a revolution in leadership is of the utmost urgency. Who among the leaders you have met best represents the ideal?

Díez-Hochleitner: First, the King of Spain, who is a very special person for me and my compatriots; his words and deeds are always respectful of the people and the environment. Among the many illustrious leaders I have been privileged to meet in my life, John F. Kennedy comes next; his picture is always displayed in our home.

Ikeda: President Kennedy humanized politics; transcending the power ethic, he believed in the power of conscience. He told us all that pessimistically considering peace impossible and unreal is defeatist, that man can be as big as he wants, and that no problem of human destiny is beyond human beings' capacity to solve it.[2] Like a fresh breath of hope in leaderless times, his words encourage us in our struggle for peace.

Díez-Hochleitner: Being appointed and seconded by UNESCO as executive secretary of the Education Task Force, in charge of a ten-year education plan for Latin America within the Alliance for Progress programme gave me a number of opportunities to meet President Kennedy during an exciting phase of history.

Ikeda: In 1960, shortly after I became president of Soka Gakkai, I received a request for an interview from President Kennedy; unfortunately his tragic assassination intervened, and I never met him. But I did meet Senator Edward Kennedy in Tokyo in January 1978, during the Cold War. I said to him, 'Human values are the important thing. International society faces a plethora of difficulties, but the Soviets and the Chinese are human beings, too. We must work hard to make international society more aware of the concept of the community of humanity.'

Senator Kennedy replied that, to promote mutual understanding among peoples, we must act in humane ways. Our humanity is our starting point; we must return to our humanity. These words evoke the nobility, courage and optimism typical of the whole Kennedy family.

Díez-Hochleitner: At a time of tension and action in Europe, I also met German Chancellor Konrad Adenauer and French President Charles de Gaulle. I met Dr Adenauer while studying for my master's degree at the Higher Engineering School in Karlsruhe, and I still find his views on democracy highly inspiring. President de Gaulle combined *la grandeur* which he always wanted for France with undeniable gravitas. Although both had open, long-term visions for closer East–West cooperation, they were too entangled in short-term, postwar problems.

Ikeda: To my way of thinking, the most important of Adenauer's and de Gaulle's achievements was overcoming the discord that had existed between France and Germany since Napoleonic times and opening the door to reconciliation and alliance. Inveterate enemies before the Second World War, within a few decades the two nations have developed a relationship in which war between them is inconceivable. This irrefutable historical fact only shows that apparently unresolvable conflicts can be resolved. This is both an admonition and a sign of hope for the future.

Díez-Hochleitner: I agree. Later, as part of my activities as an international civil servant and government official, I had the privilege of meeting many other presidents and political personalities – in Africa (Julius Nyerere), Asia (Indira Ghandi), Latin America (Belisario Betancur) and Europe (Olof Palme). I learned to value many aspects of their personalities while also identifying numerous shortcomings.

During my mandate as president, the Club of Rome organized several one-day, closed-door dialogues between three or four of these leaders and our executive committee. In most cases it quickly became clear that the meeting was strictly off-the-record, and then these apparently staunch, conceited and influential people became quite happy to accept advice, recognizing their own ignorance, limitations and uncertainties in numerous areas.

Ikeda: Your experience with various leaders reveals that the human element is far too important to be ignored during discussions of politics and systems.

Díez-Hochleitner: It is, indeed. My acquaintance with our mutual friend Mikhail S. Gorbachev, started later. With a few other members of the Club of Rome executive committee, we visited President Gorbachev at the Kremlin after he had launched perestroika and glasnost. From the very beginning, we established a most cordial and fruitful relationship. Since then, we have met on numerous occasions in Russia and elsewhere, including Spain. I followed with sympathy and admiration his pilgrimage towards democracy and later his work on global cooperation, human rights, peace and freedom. True to his ideals, he started by trying to help Communism overcome its many failures. Later he firmly led the transformation of the USSR into a democratic, free Russia. I have profound admiration for his efforts and his success.

Ikeda: Mikhail Gorbachev could have wielded power like his predecessors in the Kremlin; but, even though he realized that he also would be swept away with it, he embarked on a mission of democratization and liberalization. He once said to me, 'I know all about power. When it and politics are accompanied by unjust and immoral actions, I cannot accept them. After long consideration, I have come to believe firmly that there can be no compromise with politics devoid of morality.' Gorbachev crushed the foundations of the Kremlin power structure; his emergence on the stage of history was most fortunate.

Díez-Hochleitner: Now it is my turn to ask who among the many leaders you have met impressed you most.

Ikeda: Among leaders from Asia, I must cite the premier of the People's Republic of China, Zhou Enlai, whom I met while he was hospitalized in Beijing in December 1974. Although he was incurably ill, he found time for a young man like me. He was a resolute revolutionary, a refined diplomat and a clear-sighted man of business. In one physical body, he embodied a combination of penetrating historical wisdom and profound devotion to the good of others. Furthermore, he helped guide China to its present state of prosperous development by battling the Gang of Four and protecting Deng Xiaoping and the younger generation of leaders. Without Zhou Enlai, one of the most outstanding Asian leaders of the twentieth century, China would not be as prosperous and stable as it is now: without a stable, prosperous China, Asia cannot prosper.

Díez-Hochleitner: I cannot help feeling that, in comparison with the charismatic figures we have been discussing – people of ideals and willpower – most leaders today are only mediocre.

Ikeda: Unfortunately, I must agree. Individuals find it increasingly hard to display leadership capabilities and set new courses now that politics, economics, science and education have become over-sized and intensely specialized. Ironically, however, these conditions are precisely the reasons why leaders now and in the future need to be extraordinarily capable and courageous.

Personally, I believe a poetic spirit is one of the essential characteristics of good leaders in the new era. I think of this spirit in terms of what I call the poetic eye: the eye of one who has experienced great literature and has honed his or her own powers of expression. The eye of the social sciences analyses and interprets major currents in human history. The poetic eye draws on the accumulated wisdom of the world's literary culture and foresees the optimum nature of society with long-term vision based on respect for the universe and the dignity of life.

As the Swiss psychiatrist Carl Gustav Jung thought, ours is a time when organizational designation takes precedence over the individual human entity and when individual moral responsibility is being replaced by national rationality.[3] In such an era, leaders lack the poetic eye and the literary eye to discern the irreplaceable dignity of each individual. I call the few politicians who have these traits 'poet-politicians'.

Such politicians accept responsibility for what they say and, through lively discourse, they inspire in people the courage to accept challenges. The politicians we have just been discussing are brilliant examples of what I mean.

Díez-Hochleitner: I like your reference to poet-politicians very much. Poetry and philosophy are, in my view, the very peak of spiritual creativity. The ideal politician is someone who is honestly devoted to serving society by ensuring free elections and the active participation of civil society in the implementation of the particular projects and general goals promised in the programme of his political party. I consider my close friend former President of Colombia (1982–6) Dr Belisario Betancur such a person.

In the future, politicians must ideally demonstrate to society the implications of short-term programmes and their medium- and long-term consequences in what I call 'anticipatory democracy'.

Ikeda: That is a very important point. Today the discrepancies and contradictions between what politicians offer as mid- and long-term programmes and the short-term policies they actually implement, are greater than they have ever been before. A truly effective leader must resolutely reform the situation at hand while always keeping the long-term vision in mind.

While passionately protecting the dignity of individual lives, the politician must be fully aware of progress in the social sciences. In addition, he must advance steadily towards peaceful coexistence for all humanity, keeping his eye fixed on the mid- and long-term prospects.

Doing no more than effecting a change from nation state to global governance would be meaningless. Politics and politicians must take as their mainstays respect for the dignity of life, sound prospects and the powers to implement them, as well as eloquence to inspire in people a sense of community and courage. This is why I advocate a revolution in leadership: without it, we cannot save the planet.

Díez-Hochleitner: I agree – you have touched on the topic of global governance, and I am concerned by the state of governance at the present time, and by what moves we must initiate to improve it. We must bear in mind the numerous strata of governance: governmental and administrative structure, business and private organizations.

Ikeda: In searching for the best kind of transnational government, after the Second World War, Albert Einstein and Bertrand Russell spoke of the need for a world government or a world federation, but their ideas have proved difficult to realize and unlikely to be achieved. During the 1990s, the idea of global governance appeared, whereby diverse organizations without overall supervision, including nation states, could come together to discuss problems and create a kind of global management network. This would amount to a kind of governance without government; that is, governance by network, without centralized authority. But such an arrangement can hardly avoid reflecting power relations among nations at the time.

A number of points must be taken into consideration if we are to arrive at a just and responsible global governance. First, the United Nations must be its crux; it must be reformed and strengthened. Next, the rule of law must be systematized step by step. Getting the International Criminal Court on track is an important test case in this process. Third, governance must be built on popular solidarity.

Another vital issue is that we must not leave everything up to leaders: we must expand the circle of global citizens who are profoundly concerned about humanity-wide values and who have a sense of responsibility to future generations. In this context, the Club of Rome and SGI see eye to eye. The ordinary people are the creators of history; cultivating them is certain to bring forth outstanding leaders that will provide the driving force for the revolution in leadership.

Díez-Hochleitner: I agree. Stressing the importance of this point, the Club of Rome pays great attention to business and businessmen. In my thirty years' experience in dealing with big businesses, I have found many negative aspects. Lacking social awareness and social responsibility, they have often been willing to destroy the natural environment and cared little about their employees and stockholders. However, they are gradually coming to understand environmental issues better and to devote part of their profits to pertinent foundations, NGOs and economic-aid organizations.

Ikeda: Yes. No business enterprise can fail to take the environment into consideration, and some of them are taking this as a chance to increase the value of their business. The Club of Rome's *The Limits to Growth* was certainly a turning point in this transformation of attitudes because it showed consumers that the environment cannot be used as a limitless storehouse of resources and that, if consumers change, businesses must follow suit.

An initiative by former UN Secretary-General Kofi Annan, called the 'Global Compact', calls for combined efforts on the part of the United Nations, business and NGOs to secure the financial resources and regulate the actions of transnational corporations regarding human rights, working conditions and the environment. For their part, businesses find the project advantageous because it shows them in a positive light, cooperating with the United Nations in the name of human rights and the environment.

Like it or not, transnational corporations are important players in international society. Some people criticize the Global Compact for allowing businesses to make use of UN authority with impunity. Nonetheless, I hope that in the years to come this kind of loose union will gradually become more common.

Díez-Hochleitner: The media are another topic that must be included in any discussion about global society. Human beings have a fundamental right to a free flow of appropriate, accurate and unmanipulated information. A globalized information flow allows all kinds of constructive possibilities and prevents the use of globalization for the exclusive advantage of the rich and the powerful. The unfettered flow of appropriate information has immense ethical and moral value, which is why we should set up analytical organizations to review and advise each media group to ensure that information is ethical, independent and objective.

Ikeda: Media politics are growing stronger and stronger, locally and internationally. Politicians are aware of media attention and often attempt to manage the flow of information to their own advantage. The amount of information available to all of us increases in leaps and bounds, but as the volume grows, so does the amount of false and potentially domineering information. To cope with this situation, we must inculcate media literacy in children from a very early age.

We must also consider whether the evolution of media can make us happy. Evolution typified by things like satellite broadcasting and the Internet presents two future images of globalization: the positive image points to strengthened international connections that aid the growth of global democracy, however, the darker second image suggests a surveillance society of the kind depicted by George Orwell in *Nineteen Eighty-Four*.

We should strive to realize the first image. Doing so requires us to organize information and understand it correctly. We must also realize that knowledge alone does not lead to happiness; to be happy, human beings must have the wisdom to make good use of their knowledge. Two increasingly important ways to acquire such wisdom are stimulating dialogue and reading with the aim of learning from our intellectual heritage.

TEN

World Citizens and Education

Ikeda: A world-famous educator, you have been a university professor in Spain and Colombia. You have held key positions related to educational planning, financing, administration and reform at the OAS, UNESCO and the World Bank. In addition, you have advised many governments on educational policies and have been responsible for major educational reform in Spain. Because of your experience in this field, in this chapter of our dialogue, I should like to focus on education.

Díez-Hochleitner: I, too, should like to make education the salient theme of this part of our discussion because I know it is a topic of utmost concern to you.

Ikeda: You and I have had frequent opportunities to talk about education. In a dialogue in 1992, we spoke of the need for individual human revolution as essential to the global revolution, which reminds me of something Aurelio Peccei once pointed out. He said that solving our complex problems requires that people alter their selfish patterns of action, and to this end he proposed a new humanism and the human revolution. He said that, though growth is limited, there are no limitations on learning; external natural resources are finite, but internal human riches are infinite.

83

He believed that we must develop the wisdom to make good use of our knowledge.

Sharing his ideas, you have said that we must understand where we have come from and where we are headed. You believe that pathology in humanity is the cause of the illness of the Earth. As these thoughts clearly illustrate, individual human revolutions are the answer, and education is an indispensable element in the process.

Díez-Hochleitner: Having received an honorary doctorate in 1994 from Soka University in Tokyo, I have had the privilege of observing some of your educational work around the world. Soka University of America (SUA) seems to represent a culmination of that work.

Ikeda: Thank you for your kind words. In the summer of 2004, Soka University of America welcomed its first senior class; we now have students in all four undergraduate years.

America sets great store by education; on the occasion of our opening, the event was covered by more than forty papers across the United States. The *New York Times* ran a special article on Soka University of America, using phrases like 'reaches skyward above the Pacific', 'an architectural and educational marvel' and 'Soka University of America has a grand dream.'

Soka University of America held its first commencement ceremonies in May 2005. More than thirty of the one hundred graduates qualified for graduate school. This percentage is on a par with such famous institutions as Yale and the University of California at Berkeley.

Díez-Hochleitner: That is an astounding achievement for a university that has only recently opened.

Ikeda: American graduate schools are reluctant to accept students from institutions lacking a record of achievements. However, our students are readily accepted because they possess high scholastic calibre, open-mindedness, and passion to contribute to society.

Speaking at the graduation ceremony, Jack W. Peltason, a prominent figure in American education and former president of

84

the University of California, said that, even with his long years of experience in higher education, he found the high quality of education Soka University of America offered very impressive. He also said that the first graduating class bore witness to the passion of the faculty and the eagerness of the students to make contributions to humanity.

We greatly appreciate this kind of support, which we enjoy from you, too, and from many people throughout the world.

Díez-Hochleitner: I think that being able to establish a university in such a prestigious place as California shows that your organization has earned respect and praise and enjoys amicable relations with the community.

How do you explain the great attention devoted to Soka University of America?

Ikeda: As of 2005, the student body consisted of people from more than thirty countries representing many different nationalities, ethnic groups, languages and religions; all of them are treated completely equally. The institution attracts wide attention because it cultivates citizens of the world and, most of all, because its education is humanistic and student-centred.

Symbolically, the student accommodation commands the best views; faculty and students share one dining hall; the president's office is the same size as the offices of other faculty members. In such happy circumstances, where they breathe the air of human rights, students naturally grow into citizens of the world.

Dr Thomas Lindsay, provost of the University of Dallas, who sympathizes profoundly with our student-centred education and strict observance of respect for peace, human rights and life, has said, 'The university hopes to contribute by inculcating in the souls of its students the means of a global humanistic perspective on the world. As a student educated in the West, I was impressed because I found at SUA an intersection between the purposes of Soka (value-creation) education and the Western liberal arts tradition.'

Díez-Hochleitner: Generally, high-ranking university officials have very few chances for dialogue with teachers, let alone with students. By bringing students and faculty closer together in a new student-centred tradition, Soka University of America may be taking the lead in a university revolution.

Ikeda: I believe that you, too, have founded institutes of higher learning.

Díez-Hochleitner: Yes, but always as part of a public educational system aimed mainly at equal opportunities, life-long education and educational excellence.

First, in Colombia (1955–7), as part of my design for a five-year educational plan, I promoted a number of new universities, among them the Technical University in Pereira, which bears my name.

In 1968, thanks to an initiative on the part of the then crown prince, I returned to Spain to conduct a major overall educational reform on the basis of the General Education Bill (Ley General de Educación) of 1970. By that time, as student revolts in the United States and France inspired Spaniards to press for change, the Franco regime was inexorably doomed. I was appointed under-secretary of state in the Ministry of Education and Science.

I am extremely happy to have been able to contribute to my homeland by bringing about badly needed, drastic reforms in Spanish education in the days preceding the transition to democracy.

Part of my work was the founding of five autonomous pilot universities (two of them polytechnic universities) in Bilbao, Madrid, Barcelona and Valencia. The College of Agriculture created at the same time in Palencia also bears my name. Our main resources, however, were devoted to junior and senior high schools, primary schools and to teacher training colleges.

Ikeda: I thoroughly understand the great joy of overcoming hardships to found a university through one's own efforts. Many people opposed my founding the Soka junior and senior high schools – the foundation of 'value-creating' education – at a time when the Soka Gakkai financial situation was very tight. But I insisted that the two mainstays of character development are education and religion, and religion without education is merely self-righteousness. My own mentor Josei Toda eagerly wished to make Mr Makiguchi's philosophy flourish throughout the world, and I wanted to satisfy his wish.

Díez-Hochleitner: The world was in turmoil when Soka University of America was founded.

Ikeda: Yes. The first class matriculated in August 2001, not long before the horrendous terrorist attacks of 11 September. The students were profoundly affected by the events, especially since they were eager to make the new century an era of peace. On the evening of the day of the attacks, the students invited local citizens to come to the campus to join them in a memorial service for the victims.

The next day, a local senior high-school boy sent an e-mail to Soka University of America saying that, though his heart had been filled with hatred at first, attending the memorial and hearing what people had to say calmed him down and made him realize the importance of peace.

This indicates how vital it is to use dialogue to make people share the desire for peace. Pivotal to achieving this is the extent to which we can expand pacifist solidarity. Now, having overcome the shock of that day, our students are even more passionately engaged in the pacifist struggle.

Díez-Hochleitner: Hardships make people stronger. We all look forward to the great contributions that Soka University of America and Toda Institute for Global Peace and Policy Research in Hawaii will make to world peace.

At this point, I should like to learn more about the origins of your philosophy of Soka (value-creating) education.

Ikeda: Too many people today have distorted ideas of the purpose of education, and this causes a great deal of trouble. Today education generally strives exclusively to force students into moulds useful to industrial society, whereas, by its very nature, it ought to enable each student to fulfil their diverse potential.

On the basis of specific social values, contemporary education is narrowly restricted and caught up in facile standardization. People or projects that fail to fit standard patterns are often cut off and discarded with devastating effects on teachers and students. In the attempt to break free of these restraints, value-creating education insists that society must serve the needs of education, instead of the other way round.

Tsunesaburo Makiguchi's philosophy is the starting point of our educational approach. At a time when militaristic indoctrination raged throughout the land, Mr Makiguchi boldly declared the goal of education to be to make children happy. For value-creating education, the primary consideration is the happiness of the children we have in front of us. If we concentrate on attaining this goal, the nature of education will change dramatically. Responsibility obviously falls not only on educators, but also on families, communities and society as a whole, including its political and economic aspects.

Díez-Hochleitner: I see. That is a very important point. In my view, education and learning remain no more than information unless educators (parents, teachers and, I hope, society at large) set examples that pass on ethical and moral values to students and teach the need for consistency between proclaimed values and everyday behaviour. This I call 'pedagogy through example'.

Ikeda: You have taken part in many different international educational activities. For example, at the early age of 28 you were director of educational planning as well as general coordinator at the Education Ministry of Colombia.

Díez-Hochleitner: Yes, after having studied the sciences, technology and management, I dedicated my life to education. I worked in technical and vocational education first, followed by educational policies, expansion, quality, financing and administration. In all these endeavours I have striven to make the greatest contributions to education that I could.

As a 24-year-old university teacher, I travelled to Colombia, where I was later made director of educational planning. With financial assistance from the World Bank and later with the help of the Alliance for Progress programme launched by President J. F. Kennedy, we succeeded in conducting some important projects and reforms in the educational sector within Colombia and in many other Latin American countries.

I returned to Spain as inspector-general of technical education, but eight months later forces rigidly opposed to reform threatened us. Realizing that we were in actual physical danger, the Colombian minister of education appointed me to a post at the level of a vice-minister in charge of preparing a five-year educational plan, and so I returned to Colombia.

Ikeda: Virulent opposition to people who set out to do great good is a given of human society. In the face of such opposition, you stood by your beliefs and opened a path to universal education. At an early age, you became director of educational planning and general coordinator of the Education Ministry of Colombia. These were great responsibilities for one so young – what kinds of difficulties did they impose?

Díez-Hochleitner: When I was young, I regarded suffering as a normal part of life. If I had been much older, I might have come to entertain doubts, but great ability to stand up against hardships is inherent in youth. This is the product of hope, or courage, sometimes resulting from youthful innocence. I have suffered mainly because of the sufferings of beloved family members and friends: undue pressures and menaces from extremists from both ends of the political spectrum as well as from terrorists (like ETA, the Basque separatist movement) have caused suffering for me personally.

Ikeda: I see. As a result of your great achievements in Colombian reform, you were included in UNESCO's global educational planning team.

Díez-Hochleitner: Yes. Having been in charge of preparing the substantial documentation and organizing a Pan-American Conference in Washington DC on educational planning based on the Colombian pilot five-year education plan, in 1958 I introduced the educational planning programme in UNESCO at the request of the then director-general. The UNESCO General Conference chose it as the highest priority activity of its education sector in 1959.

I carried out technical assistance missions in many countries, helped to establish regional training centres for educational planning, administration and reform, and was in charge of organizing regional conferences between ministers of education and ministers of economics, to introduce educational plans and reforms in their respective countries.

During one of these regional conferences for Asia, I learned something interesting about cultural differences. It was in fact my first visit to an Asian country; as I was addressing the inaugural session of Asian ministers in Karachi in December 1959, I noticed that many audience members were shaking their heads from left to right. Though they greeted my talk with a round of applause, I thought with disappointment that they had disagreed with my message. I whispered my concern to an Indian colleague (UNESCO's Deputy Director-General Malcolm Adiseshiah) sitting besides me. Laughingly, he explained that I had been mistaken: the head shaking had not signalled disagreement, rather it was the sign of approval. When he told the audience of my error, they demonstrated their sympathy with further rounds of loud applause. In my great admiration for them, thereafter I frequently referred to this incident when I addressed other Asian groups.

Ikeda: That only goes to show how customs and cultures differ. You have achieved great things and made important contributions by training people to become global citizens.

Díez-Hochleitner: You are too generous. Through such things as your proposals, you too have always advocated education from a global viewpoint.

Ikeda: In my proposals for 2004, I highlighted education as an area requiring maximum effort for the sake of peace. Education is the key to happiness; it is the basis on which peace can flourish. It is the foundation that allows us to bring to fruition the capacity to work for our own happiness and the happiness of others. In the world today, 860 million adults are said to be illiterate; schooling is unavailable to 120 million children. Measures to rectify this situation are urgently needed because world development targets cannot be met without progress in education.

However, many countries lack the funds to provide even primary education. International cooperation is required to break down obstacles in their way; the United Nations aims to make primary education available as widely as possible. To support its efforts, I advocate reinforcing the international system of monetary cooperation in the form of a global primary-education fund.

Díez-Hochleitner: In my view, investing in a fund to expand at least primary education in the developing nations is more valuable than investing in economic growth and will certainly have longer-lasting results. I have always acted on this conviction.

You insist that, instead of being limited to specific groups, education must be universal. Similarly, I have always promoted high-quality education, equal opportunities and life-long education that generates sustainable economic growth and cultural values. It should be available to absolutely everybody because it contributes to good health and higher living standards, thanks to people becoming more productive and more responsible.

Achieving this is the goal we promote in a variety of ways: for instance, we provide information and generate a strong sense of solidarity by setting up information centres in thousands of rural farming villages and connecting them to the world by means of radio and the Internet. For its future globalization, education must encompass all fields and aspects of scientific culture and cultural science. The full power of education is demonstrated when it approaches all subjects simultaneously and holistically. What are your thoughts on the education of people to become global citizens as a foundation of a war-free world?

Ikeda: Merely making teaching more widely available will not create the proper ground for peaceful coexistence; the quality of education must also be taken into consideration. Education that incites conflicts between nations or promotes discrimination among ethnic groups can only aggravate mistrust and hatred.

As the American journalist Norman Cousins said, 'A casual attitude toward human hurt and pain is the surest sign of educational failure.'[1]

Díez-Hochleitner: Exactly. Dramatic increases in information or even knowledge do not necessarily bring wisdom. In Spain today, where educational quality is a topic of great concern, more people are studying more material, and larger numbers of young people are receiving higher education than ever before. There is, however, a crisis associated with this knowledge. A society that has absorbed vast amounts of knowledge as quickly as possible is a by-product of our immense success. Our breath is virtually taken away by huge amounts of suffocating information that cannot be assimilated.

To become knowledge, information must be assimilated; we solve problems by acquiring, classifying and selecting it. But vast amounts of knowledge and the cultivation of that knowledge do not necessarily lead to wisdom; indeed augmented knowledge without understanding can lead to horrors like Nazi Germany. Although they knew how to employ knowledge for the purpose of mass killing, the Nazis had no idea how to employ wisdom for the sake of harmonious coexistence. They put knowledge and education to use in creating a compulsory culture of domination.

Ikeda: Knowledge can be a double-edged sword. Many knowledgeable Japanese people glorified the Second World War.

A truly good education teaches how to use knowledge to produce wisdom and how to develop innate human potential. In the years to come, education must encourage people to be aware of their world citizenship.

Díez-Hochleitner: It is impossible to discuss educational reform without taking into consideration reforms in local neighbourhoods and communities. As José Ortega y Gasset said, we must begin with fundamentals.

A good world citizen must start by being a good family member, a good fellow worker or professional, and a good member of the local community. Starting with fundamentals of this kind has a great impact on deep reform; this relates to your idea that a single individual can change the environment, region, nation and even the whole world. It is from this standpoint that you and I are discussing the future of globalized education. As I said earlier, global education must include all fields and aspects; that is, scientific culture and cultural sciences. Education shows its essential importance when it covers all phenomena and yet remains always aware of the bigger picture.

Ikeda: The fundamental part is the revolution within a single human being. Human rights and environmental education are essential to the cultivation of global citizens to build a society of peaceful coexistence.

Some time ago, I addressed a message to the United Nations recommending the designation of a 'Decade of Human Rights Education for Peace' as a sequel to its 'Decade for Human Rights Education' (1995–2004). Such a project should take into consideration issues confronting humanity, like peace and poverty, while focusing on children, who must bear the burden of proceeding generations. The project should also concentrate on human rights education for the creation of a global society of peace and symbiosis.

In this context, SGI cooperates with other NGOs and national governments. As concern over human rights intensifies, in January 2005 the United Nations initiated its World Programme for Human Rights Education; this promotes efforts to develop citizens of the world, an undertaking that we must support.

Díez-Hochleitner: Education must do more than evoke human creative powers enabling individuals and groups to discover the mysteries of nature with deeper understanding; it must teach love as well. If I know a person, I can love that person, similarly, a person with knowledge should love that knowledge. Knowledge and scientific technology should be used, not for war, destruction and pollution, but for peace and sustainable social and humane development. I believe that education on the environment can revolutionize individuals´ attitudes towards nature and ensure a harmonious relationship between man and nature.

Ikeda: I agree entirely. Adults who teach human rights and environmental education must live in ways that demonstrate concern with human rights and the environment.

In a dialogue he and I are conducting, Dr M. S. Swaminathan, president of the Pugwash Conferences and proponent of the Evergreen Revolution, said environmental education must supply instruction in sustainable lifestyles that economize on natural resources. It runs counter to sustainability, however, when classrooms teach the importance of the environment while television stimulates greater consumption of goods or when governments pour vast sums into military budgets. Observing adults behaving in this duplicitous fashion, children come to regard environmental problems as just something that may turn up in school examinations.

In addition, Dr Swaminathan believes that teaching non-violence is the most important aspect of environmental education.

Díez-Hochleitner: Education can solve many of the big problems we will face in the future. To put its power to full use, we must ask ourselves the following questions. Do we respect and care for life and nature? Are we respectful and tolerant towards other people? Do we manifest solidarity with the poor of all countries? Are we tainted with consumerism that has crept up on us unawares?

Ikeda: Those are important points. Today non-violence pertains to more than avoiding physically violent behaviour. Behind the discrimination, oppression, poverty and human rights violations causing many of our problems, institutionalized violence extends everywhere from the home to international society. In relation to nature it takes the form of environmental pollution; in the human realm it causes infringements of human rights. True non-violence is possible only if we overcome structural violence. Making people citizens of the world depends on education on peace, human rights and environmental matters. These three mainstays are, in fact, integrated.

Díez-Hochleitner: Ethical and moral values are a priority. However, in what ways can we teach new lifestyles that over-come structural violence?

Ikeda: Respect for human life must be the foundation of all education. The dignity and uniqueness of life is inherent in individual personalities and in the entire human race. Humanity depends on the natural world; when we respect humanity, we must revere and learn from nature. Recognizing the dignity of the individual must result in mutual recognition and respect: recognizing the absolute fundamental dignity of human life brings diverse values to flower by encouraging people everywhere to learn from each other on an equal footing.

Previously, humanity – especially in the industrial nations – has tended to give precedence to economic and technological values. The essential thing now, however, is for all of us to regard the dignity of human life as the most fundamental value of all. On this basis, we must allow diverse cultural and social values to exist side by side and use dialogue as a means of coordinating them all.

ELEVEN

Renaissance of Religion and Spirituality

Ikeda: Up to this point, we have discussed numerous problems currently confronting humanity and ways of dealing with them. Now I should like to round off the discussion with thoughts about the future outlook for the planet and the extremely important role that spiritual culture may play in it.

Díez-Hochleitner: I could not agree more. As you know, I was raised as a member of a Catholic family; while far from setting an example, I have tried to behave and be true to my faith. But for me it has always been most important not only to be *tolerant* towards other beliefs and cultures, but also, and even more important, to *respect* everyone who acts honestly and consistently in line with their background and aims. Furthermore, I try to learn from others to enrich my spirit and intellect, while contributing somehow to their well-being, advancement and happiness. From this perspective, as I respect and admire you, I should like to ask you about the Buddhist viewpoint on the theme you propose; on this subject, I am certainly the one to listen and learn.

Ikeda: You have the modesty of a philosophical person who acts with conviction. Certain features have pervaded our dialogue:

97

first of all humanity; second is education, which is the optimum means for refining our humanity; third is the culture that supports and directs education.

As you know, the English word 'culture' derives from the Latin verb *colere*, to till or cultivate. We cultivate the individual human being by tilling the fields of intellect, emotions and thought. On a larger scale, we improve culture by cultivating society. The idea of culture inspires expectations for seeking and manifesting inner psychological and spiritual values.

Díez-Hochleitner: I agree. When superficial values are skimmed away from human culture and the more essential values examined, we discover shared principles.

Ikeda: The English word 'civilization' connotes urbanization; that is, a device for establishing functioning cities supported by the power of civilization. In discussions of civilizations, external and material aspects assume great importance; human beings have created and enjoyed the results of many civilizations in different regions; but behind their prosperity has been a painful venom. The rise and fall of civilizations have been discussed by many historians, including Arnold J. Toynbee, with whom I published a dialogue. These scholars have proposed various learned theories, but I believe that inner human culture and the civilization that promotes development in the social environment on which our real lives depend are mutually dependent.

Díez-Hochleitner: Culture is extremely important because it makes civilization possible.

Ikeda: While interacting to some extent, past civilizations preserved local independence. In the modern age of globalization, however, civilization extends to the whole planet and to all humanity, and developments in transport and communication networks provide the major impetus. Characteristically, modern Western techno-scientific civilization has had a tremendous impact on globalization: the ubiquitous presence of certain commercial products and far-flung locations of production all over the world make this immediately apparent. In the material and economic dimensions, modern Western civilization has even made incursions into ancient and venerable Chinese, Hindu and Islamic cultures. It has penetrated the core realms of spiritual culture, transforming lifestyles and altering values and views on nature. These developments arouse concern about the destruction of the social environments and foundations on which unique traditions and cultures rest. For instance, hundreds of languages that support culture, and propagate it for posterity, face the danger of extinction.

Díez-Hochleitner: Civilization today gives the impression of being something enforced; the mass communication media have made Americanization the dominant lifestyle model.

Ikeda: That is why, not only in other parts of the world, but also in the West itself, more and more people are calling for re-examination, restoration, respect and protection of distinctive local cultures.

Díez-Hochleitner: The important thing is to recognize different cultures as civilizations and to appreciate and learn from them. We must overcome discrimination or misinformation that sees some cultures as uncivilized. We must never attempt to subordinate other cultures.

Ikeda: I agree. Mutual respect and learning from each other are essential for the truly civilized. Nonetheless, some people who are avid about respecting and protecting traditions and cultures react in emotional and destructive ways against globalization; in some instances the reaction sparks the rise of destructive and fundamentalist movements.

Díez-Hochleitner: The crisis of value systems, notably in the form of moral relativism, is an issue to which the Club of Rome is currently giving precedence. We can no longer permit ourselves to be good people, philanthropists, champions of justice and fantasists who say one thing and do another. Our words and deeds must agree and must move to contribute to the well-being of others. We must begin by examining and regulating ourselves and then expand our efforts outwards.

Ikeda: Self-righteousness only generates new discord; tolerant, universal values are the important thing. Allowing globalization to lapse into mere standardization amounts to destroying the rich cultural diversity that humanity has created over the ages.

Díez-Hochleitner: Though it may be efficient, homogenization has serious faults in terms of crisis management.

Ikeda: Carried away on the tide of the current time, individuals find it hard to orient themselves; this is another great contemporary crisis. In my view, in the years to come, satisfying spiritual or existential values must become the moral axis of global civilization; it will be more important than ever before. Even in the sphere of economics, we must deal with spiritual as well as with material poverty. As an indication of the increasing urgency of establishing order within ourselves – our inner cosmos – the World Health Organization (WHO) is now stressing the importance of developing and maintaining good spiritual health.

Díez-Hochleitner: World peace is unattainable unless we have inner peace. But the problem is difficult because the inner cosmos, in other words the soul, of each individual is a world in itself, calling out for a religious and spiritual renaissance.

Ikeda: Since time immemorial, religion has been the source of fundamentally satisfying spiritual values. But old-fashioned religions no longer completely satisfy human needs; something new is required. The human thirst for religion creates the need for the religious and spiritual renaissance you mention. The spiritual culture of the future must be more than a mere rehashing of past heritages. I believe humanity has arrived at the stage for a new spiritual leap forward.

Díez-Hochleitner: The soul, or inner cosmos, longs for the internal manifestation of philosophy and value systems, the noblest things human beings are capable of.

Ikeda: The German philosopher Karl Jaspers (1883–1969) was acutely aware of the need for a spiritual-cultural revival. In what he defined as the axial age (the time between 800 and 200 BCE) the world witnessed the emergence of thinkers who created the framework of human spiritual culture: Laozi, Confucius, Mozi, Xuangzi and Liezi in China; Shakyamuni and the six non-Buddhist teachers in India; the Hebrew prophets from Elijah to Deutero-Isaiah; and Greek philosophers like Socrates and Plato. Jaspers also posited a second axial age in the vanguard of the modern techno-scientific age; I am especially interested in this possibility.

Díez-Hochleitner: It is a very important point that deserves discussing.

Ikeda: In 1949, Jaspers formulated his intellectually brilliant idea that human history has taken two 'deep breaths', or progressed in two great bursts. The first started with what he called a Promethean Age of technical mastery and flowed through the high point of ancient culture, breathing life into the axial age and subsequent times.[1]

More than a half a century after Jaspers wrote this, his idea of a second axial age is urgently required. A New Promethean Age has brought scientific technology, including nuclear power, which is confronting humanity with the possible crises of either instant annihilation of the Earth or extermination through slow poisoning.

Díez-Hochleitner: As you know, Aristotle pointed to melancholy (a mental condition of extreme feelings of transitoriness from which one might construct a spiritual-cultural revival) as the very basis of philosophy. Therefore, it is not surprising that Jaspers, who was previously a clinical psychiatrist, also focused on melancholy.

The possibility of a second axial age and world union, which Jaspers predicted after the Second World War and the horrors of the Nazis, is consistent with the long-term developments of human history. However, this is only true if, in the face of the increasingly serious mismanagement of technology and environmental resources, humanity survives through the millennium. The major risk arises from prolonged actions running counter to commonly accepted ethical values, human rights, duties and moral values derived from religious beliefs.

Ikeda: Now I should like to consider whether spiritual and philosophical foundations can ensure sustainable prosperity in the future. I believe that respect for the dignity of life must become a universally recognized value. The inviolability of life is a basic ethical tenet of most religions. Prohibition against taking life is one of the five major Buddhist precepts, as well as one of the Ten Commandments received by Moses. Many other religions also forbid both mortal harm to the physical body and violence, including structural violence resulting in spiritual and existential death. In general, religions condemn acts that hinder the manifestation of life's limitless possibilities.

Díez-Hochleitner: The Club of Rome has declared itself to be anthropocentric and, since our survival depends on the planet Earth, nature-friendly. Personally, I consider humanity – each individual human being – the most sacred thing on Earth. Because I can judge no one, I make no exceptions for specific circumstances; that is, it is not important whether people are believers or non-believers, what philosophy or reasoning they have, and so on. Wisdom based on a worldwide cultural heritage requires us to recognize human dignity and the dignity of life, both individual and communal.

Ikeda: Human wisdom, including that of world religions, urges us to promote both individual satisfaction and prosperity and the common prosperity and betterment of all.

Díez-Hochleitner: In a truly praiseworthy fashion, you show the importance of respecting and learning from the past. In this way, you contribute far more to the world than you can learn from it. Your tireless efforts to answer vital questions encourage people and stimulate their desire to learn more about the Buddhist principles on which your own thoughts and deeds are based. This is true for me as well: while remaining loyal to my lifelong faith, I am willing to enrich myself with your wisdom and to exercise all-encompassing respect for other spiritual and existential values.

Ikeda: Thank you for your generous words of praise; please allow me to express my respect for your sincere desire to learn.

The Buddhist scriptures teach the importance of diversity, notably in the metaphor of the different trees: though all different, the cherry, the plum, the peach and the apricot are wonderfully beautiful in themselves. Similarly, each living thing has individual value that it must strive to manifest fully.

Díez-Hochleitner: The internal human cosmos (the soul) is in a healthy state when love leads it to search for things useful to both others and the self. Concentration on self-interest, on the other hand, leads to degradation and perversion. Instead of ignorance and egoism, wisdom and solidarity should be our guiding devices.

Ikeda: Exactly. Mahayana Buddhism teaches that the manifestation of internal values depends on altruistic actions. According to the scriptures, life is most precious and should be respected more than anything else in the universe. Nichiren, whom we revere, describes a Buddha – an ideal person – as one endowed with the three virtues of sovereign, teacher and parent. Enlightened to the fundamental law, such a person manifests his or her potential while striving to protect, improve and cultivate the limitless values of all other life forms.

Tsunesaburo Makiguchi sought to realize the so-called 'great good'; the most valuable way of living, which concurs with the fundamental law governing the whole universe and individual life. My own mentor Josei Toda pointed out the dynamic, harmonious and creative evolution of the universe itself and called the process of all the phenomena in the cosmos 'compassionate action'. He made the profound observation that respect and compassion for the life of the self and the other correspond with the fundamental cosmic law.

Díez-Hochleitner: Very impressive visions, all of them. I especially appreciate Josei Toda's reference to the process of all phenomena as compassionate action. The monotheistic religions also speak of God's compassion. I believe we must be suspicious of any action that is not inspired by compassion or love.

Ikeda: Some of the world's best intellects – Pierre Teilhard de Chardin, Rabindranath Tagore, Albert Einstein, Victor Frankl and others – have suggested a fundamental force behind cosmic development. Norman Cousins, who has been called the conscience of America and with whom I shared a dialogue, has written that the idea of humanity in the cosmos fires the imagination, shakes our sense of wonder, opens the door to expanded human potential and reveals a future in which human wisdom confronts infinity.[2]

Knowing that we human beings are born in the depths of the immense cosmos generates awe in the face of the eternal, infinite universe; knowing the limitless potential of humanity opens the door to a magnificent future.

In relation to the cosmic 'mission', the famous American astronomer Carl Sagan (1934–96) wrote, 'Our loyalties are to the species and the planet. We speak for Earth. Our obligation to survive is owed not just to ourselves but also to that Cosmos, ancient and vast, from which we spring.'[3] The survival of each of us is not merely for our own sakes, but for the sake of the universe as well. Sagan called survival a 'mission'. He attributed much of our current ecological catastrophe to grasping for short-term gains and 'an awesome blindness'. He called for a sense of historical continuity, a discourse on a grand scale with the ancients and with the cosmos.[4]

Díez-Hochleitner: Knowing the place and responsibility of humanity within cosmic evolution is a matter of great importance. In my view, our responsibility is first and foremost to the young and to future generations. This implies equal responsibility towards our planet and, in particular, towards all species living on it.

Ikeda: That is true. We must be aware of our great cosmic mission. We require collective wisdom, research and practical measures if we are to overcome differences of race, ethnic group, nationality, culture, civilization and gender to create a brilliant future for the cosmos.

TWELVE

Competition:
For Peace and Humane Behaviour

Ikeda: We stand at the point where the path we take determines whether humanity will succeed in creating a new global civilization. What must we do to elevate current globalization to the point where it supports the kind of world civilization on which the future of humanity can rest? What conditions must culture meet to serve as a spiritual axis for such a civilization? In this final chapter of our dialogue, I hope to search for clues to the answers to these questions.

Díez-Hochleitner: The fundamentals of all human cultures reveal certain common values. Defining these essential cultural elements constitutes, in my view, the first step in the creation of an appropriate global civilization. It is to them that we must refer when converting evil into good and ensuring the survival of the best elements of humankind. In spite of historical vicissitudes and detours, on the whole, human civilization has charted an upward course. Though various criticisms can be justly made of humanity, the human spirit of self-control, our will to improve and our inherent values have led to such things as the Universal Declaration of Human Rights: proof of a tendency to improve. Unfortunately, however, at present the Universal Declaration is not being universally applied, and its noble ideas are being corrupted. Furthermore, to be really complete, the Universal Declaration of Human Rights should include the major human duties as well.

Ikeda: Certainly it is important that humanity has discovered its own intrinsic values and proclaimed them to be universal truths; unflagging efforts to realize our ideas are essential if we are to prevent the erosion of those values. Efforts must start at home, beginning with individual self-examination. A change, a renaissance, an awakening in the individual: these are the keys to the transformation of the fate of humanity as a whole. I have believed this all my life.

Díez-Hochleitner: You are quite right. Self-criticism, which needs to be more prevalent, must begin with the individual and spread to large groups, and to humanity in general. It is not enough to complain that the world is moving in the wrong direction or that certain countries, societies or cultures are doing badly; in the same way blaming politicians and governments and their failure to reform are insufficient. Instead, each individual must ask how his or her way of living can be made better; for instance, by disposing properly of such things as electrical batteries and waste paper and conserving water resources. Only when we tackle immediate issues like these can we understand what others are doing and respond with deeper caring, greater compassion and more detailed consideration. When we do this, we are qualified to speak and make demands of others; our moral influence will increase.

Ikeda: The individual who is aware of their own worth is enlightened to the importance of others as well and can act to improve society. We must fully understand the significance of individual diversity and pay attention to the universal basis on which it rests. Nichiren urged us to be aware of our responsibility for the peace and prosperity of all: 'If the nation is destroyed and people's homes are wiped out, then where can one flee for safety? If you care anything about your personal security, you should first of all pray for order and tranquility throughout the four quarters of the land . . .'.[1] Cultivation of the rich soil in which they grow is the way to enable a great diversity of flowers to bloom in all their glory.

Díez-Hochleitner: This relates to what you said in a previous chapter in connection with the metaphor of the different flowering trees: cherry, plum, peach and apricot.

Ikeda: Yes. However, as you pointed out, merely emphasizing diversity in society runs the risk of lapsing into ethical relativism. Assuring happiness for society as a whole requires a world view that provides a clear platform for heightening human worth as far as possible, by using human values. The passage on the 'Ceremony in the Air' in the Lotus Sutra, where a huge tower springs up from the Earth, teaches a world view that expresses self-respect by revealing the inner world, centred on the Buddha life, which possesses supreme dignity.

Díez-Hochleitner: In what way?

Ikeda: The Lotus Sutra writes of honouring the dignity of life through the analogy of a richly jewelled Treasure Tower that appears floating in the air above amazed spectators. It can appear anywhere and at any time; it can be here, right now. In other words, through this image the sutra can be understood to reveal what can be called the 'eternal now'. It arises from a fissure in the Earth, and the tower symbolizes the eternal truth underlying the entire cosmos. Nichiren, who practised the teachings of the Lotus Sutra in all things, identified the Treasure Tower as being each individual believer and practitioner of the sutra's essence. This is the important thing. Essentially, the lives of all people are equally endowed with dignity on a cosmic scale, which all are capable of manifesting. Furthermore, everyone should be awake to, and mindful of, the dignity in all others. The Ceremony in the Air symbolizes this truth of all life.

Díez-Hochleitner: Please explain it in greater detail.

Ikeda: In the Ceremony in the Air, Shakyamuni enters the floating Treasure Tower, from where he preaches to all life forms in the universe and an assembly of people and characters from the sutras. The assembly includes evil people such as the cousin who tried to kill Shakyamuni, Devadatta; the representative of enlightenment for women, the Dragon King's daughter; the great historical king Ajātashatru; and representatives of those who hear the teachings and those who strive for enlightenment through their own efforts, like Shakyamuni's disciples Shāriputra, Ānanda and Maudgalyāyana. In addition, many other Buddhas and Bodhisattvas with their retainers assemble from all parts of the cosmos to hear the teaching. Four leading Bodhisattvas – among them, Superior Practices, the epitome of compassionate desire to bring all people to happiness – emerge from the foundations of the universe. Because this ceremony is centred on the Treasure Tower and all life forms attend, this part of the sutra can be thought of as representing a fundamental world view expressing the dignity of all life and the freedom, equality and solidarity that derive from that universal dignity. It teaches that living beings of all conditions – kings, evil ones, daughters of dragons – can manifest their inherent worth and live truly and justly in liberty, fairness and as one.

Díez-Hochleitner: I understand the need to recognize the inherent worth of all people, but is anger, not merely with politicians and military expansionists, but also with unjust detractors, ever justified? Unjust criticism causes misery all over the world, as human dignity comes under greater attack, even in democratic nations.

Ikeda: What you say is true. People are always being subject to unjust criticism and sometimes imprisoned on false charges; I have personal experience of this. However, persecution often proves the persecuted to be in the right; Buddhists have regarded oppression as an honour. Nonetheless, as you suggest, rampant evil threats to human dignity enrage us. Buddhist scriptures teach that anger can be either good or bad.[2] It rebounds painfully on the angry person when it arises from folly; in such cases, it is self-enclosed and destructive. However, when directed against the abuse of human dignity and unjustified pain, it is a force for good; contributing to the happiness of the self and of others. As long as they are rooted in the quest for such happiness, joy, sorrow and suffering, as well as anger, are radiant creators of value; in every condition we can manifest the dignity inherent in life, create values and generate meaning in life. Each and every being is endowed with both a sense of mission and irreplaceable precious value.

Díez-Hochleitner: We can succeed in manifesting human dignity only if we make an effort to do so; we should also recognize the rights of those who are yet to be born. We must face the truth that we are at once ourselves and our environment.

Ikeda: That is true. Rejecting the idea of innate good and innate evil, Buddhism teaches that all life is capable of both good and evil. The human being can be either the epitome of cruelty and evil or the embodiment of extreme good. This dual possibility necessitates a ceaseless, inner, spiritual struggle to crush evil and develop good and bring it to the fore. The inner struggle is inseparable from the corresponding battle in external reality.

In his autobiography *The Story of My Experiments with Truth*, Mahatma Gandhi reveals himself as conscientiously combating the evil trampling on human dignity. The inner triumph of a single individual leads to the triumph of good throughout society; proving this stern truth is our role in life.

Díez-Hochleitner: After so much wrongdoing during the last century around the world, there are abundant signs of the need of a profound spiritual renewal of mankind. Even nature seems to revolt against so much misbehaviour: for example, the gigantic tsunamis in the Asian region in December 2004 may just be an alarm bell to our collective conscience, calling for a sense of proportion in our lives.

Ikeda: That disaster was so heartrending and lamentable. We, as Buddhists, offered sincere prayers for the repose of the souls of all the victims, and our SGI members in the neighbouring countries made every possible effort in their humanitarian activities to help and support the suffering people there.

Speaking of humanism, Tsunesaburo Makiguchi looked forward to the time when, transcending military and economic competition, humanity would compete on moral and humanitarian terms. Accepting the task of bringing this transition about, in my own work I have put special emphasis on peace, culture and education. Today, enlightened to their own human worth, SGI members promote the building of a peaceful, humane society in 190 countries and regions. In the years to come, our role and that of individuals and private organizations, including NGOs and non-profit organizations (NPOs), are going to become even greater than they are now. We hope to be able to expand moral and humane competition to make this a century of peace and humane behaviour throughout the world.

Díez-Hochleitner: Keeping your views in mind, let us take the first step toward the building of such a century; let us compete together for the creation of a century of peace, sustainable human and social progress, and the general flourishing of human beings in harmony with the natural environment.

APPENDIX 1

Surmounting Darkness and the Faustian Agony: Light for Twenty-First-Century Civilization

Speech delivered by Daisaku Ikeda at the Atheneo Society of Culture and Science, Madrid, 26 June 1995

It is a great honour to speak here at the Atheneo Society of Culture and Science, an institution with a proud history and rich experience. To the president, Dr Segundo López Vélez, and all the other distinguished scholars who helped make it possible, let me express my gratitude for this valuable opportunity.

Faustian Ego

Here we are, only five and a half years from the start of the twenty-first century, and the world is in a state of utter chaos. When communism collapsed, its fall seemed to ring bells signalling the start of a new act, which we thought would bring democracy onto the stage of world politics. Within a few years, however, before the act had really begun, the stage grew dark. Since then, murky clouds have covered the world, promising to bring our century to a very unhappy end.

113

As if people were not tormented enough by one ethnic or religious struggle after another, it seems that now even cultures and civilizations, which express and shape human nature itself, are ready to clash in possibly terrible conflict. So, subverting all our hopes and expectations, the demise of the Cold War system brought not the end of strife but let loose a Pandora's box of new furies.

Given our present situation, how should we prepare for the next century? One viewpoint has generated a lot of controversy, and that is the assumption that over the next hundred years society will carry on in the path already set by the scientific-industrial civilization of the modern era. But we must not think that way. It has become inescapably obvious that if we continue on the same track, developing and spreading mass-production, mass-consumption and a throwaway culture – the trademarks of modern industrial civilization – sooner or later humanity itself will perish.

Three years ago, participants at the United Nations Conference on the Environment in Rio de Janeiro pledged to pursue sustainable development as a priority. It was a good starting point from which to mobilize the best minds in the cause of the global environment and a better future. As a Buddhist, I would argue that we must examine carefully and in depth the spirit of our age – the ethos shaped in Europe, of modern civilization. We have to illuminate the depths of that ethos in order to break free of its narrow constraints and discover alternatives for living.

When I think about the big issues in human history, I often come back to the insights of the eminent Spanish philosopher, Luis Díez del Corral. Professor Corral visited Japan as a member of Spain's cultural mission thirty years ago. Through his many speeches, he left a strong impression and is remembered with respect and affection. Corral had some thought-provoking ideas about the ethos of modern civilization. In his view, that ethos must be defined not so much by the surface dimension of politics and laws, as in the French Revolution, for example, by a 'new sense of human dignity' and 'faith beyond imagining in the innate power of humans'. It means, further, the 'effective and accurate control of human existence on the earth'.[1]

Implicated here is the over-exalted Faustian ego that has been the theme of poetry, drama, music and, of course, Goethe's tragic portrayal in *Faust*. One can find the same kind of ego lying at the heart of the modern spirit, feeding the greed for knowledge, action and control, and driving modern Europe to dominate the rest of the world. Of course these form the part of the modern spirit, the ethos of modern civilization, that is its brilliance and its light, but there is another, negative part of it, the shadow. That part has reached its ultimate dead end, revealing its limitations. Corral compares modern civilization to the exhausted Faust as he passes through the 'purgatory of suffering'.[2]

To see history in these terms interests me, not because that approach challenges the premise of modern civilization, but because it is supremely dialectic. Now, as the end-of-the-century darkness grows denser, the more vigorous and – as the proliferation of cults in industrial society testifies – diverse is the popular reaction against our times and against modernization. It seems to me that we desperately need a dialectic view of history, a view that will let us distinguish rigorously between the light and shadow in modern civilization, between the positive and negative. With that clarity of vision we can ensure that the future inherits only the light and the positive.

A thoughtful study of history from the dialectical point of view, then, should indicate what part of the ethos of modern civilization should be passed on to the generations to come. Among the valuable pieces of that legacy are the eternal and universal qualities of human nature that we talk about with words such as 'progress' and 'creativity', 'challenge' and 'pioneering', 'spontaneity' and 'action', and so on. This legacy is no less than the purposeful, dynamic expression of human life, the will to renew the self as well as revitalize the environment, all the while interacting with and working upon society and nature day by day, piece by piece. To pass on that much will help determine the ethos of the twenty-first century. If indeed we wish to bequeath the light and the positive to the future, there is still the problem of how to adjust, redirect or perhaps reconstitute what are the shady, negative areas in modern civilization.

Reorbiting Civilization – Three Approaches

Buddhism has had over two millennia to accumulate a deep and timeless spiritual heritage, and I believe that heritage can be of enormous help in working out the issues that will affect civilization in the next century. I would like to share some thoughts on the Buddhist approach, examining it in terms of three concepts: autonomy, symbiosis and inner cultivation.

If we really want to improve the way things are and nudge civilization into a more positive orbit, perhaps our very first task must be to confront our lack of self-restraint. The agony of Faust was his inability to be satisfied with his lot. His tragedy was his failure to achieve mastery over self and conquer his desire to know the whole of human experience. Speaking to Mephistopheles, he expresses his restless aching to feel more, understand more:

> ... and I'm resolved my inmost being
> Shall share in what's the lot of all mankind,
> That I shall understand their heights and depths,
> Shall fill my heart with all their joys and griefs,
> And so expand my self to theirs
> And, like them, suffer shipwreck, too.[3]

He makes a pact with Mephistopheles and is transformed. Then, invincible and arrogant, he is persuaded that he has simply achieved autonomy, but in the end he pays with his own blindness and death, his soul lost.

The story of Faust is a finely wrought dramatic tragedy from the nineteenth century, revolving around the consequences of a man's belief that he need not be subject to ordinary human constraints. In this century, the eminent philosopher from your country, José Ortega y Gasset, in his trenchant critical work *The Revolt of the Masses*, made us see a world of rudderless, wandering people unable to control themselves. He pointed out that even though our era has made so many advances, people feel 'lost in their own abundance'.[4] Ortega made that observation more than a half-century ago; the situation since then has shown no sign of changing for the better.

Modern civilization has roots in the separation in Europe of civil society and Church authority. Emerging from the Church's embrace, that civilization reached its peak in the twentieth century; so did fascism and communism. The irony is overwhelming that the very autonomy of modern civilization, achieved through liberation from religious domination, should be so compromised in the same century by the rampages of violent ideologies that arrogated to themselves quasi-religious authority.

True Victory – Over Yourself

In Buddhist thought, spiritual states such as peace, deliverance and meditative concentration are supremely important. Each state has a different significance, but they all teach us how to order our inner world. Thus the Buddhist concept of autonomy, in the sense of 'self-rule', is, as a mode of conduct, prime among all other modes of living one's life. Without the autonomy of an ordered self, everything one does is like a castle built on sand. The sutras contain countless passages relating to this theme, but consider these: 'Always behave as you teach others to behave. Only the person who can order his own conduct can order the conduct of another. It is indeed difficult to control the self,'[5] and 'The supreme victor is not the one who defeats a million enemies in battle, but the one who conquers himself.'[6]

The intent of these and many other teachings like them is to foster autonomy or 'self-order'. This Buddhist idea is slightly different from the modern ethos, which took shape when the spell of religion over European civilization was broken. Like the modern ethos, Buddhist teaching also encourages self-certainty and self-containment, but there is a clear distinction between Faustian self-conceit and what we might call the Buddhist scheme for autonomy, which, particularly in his later years, Shakyamuni increasingly invoked in terms of reliance upon self and reliance upon the Law.

One of Shakyamuni's last teachings reads, 'Be yourself a sandbank, and lean upon yourself, not others. Make the Law a sandbank, and depend upon truth, not others.'[7] In other words, to order the self, you must rely only on your own unbending self, not influenced by other people or events. To build a firm, resilient self, you have to cast off arrogance and dogmatism and rely only on the Law. Then, in the Buddhist design of things, autonomy is possible. The main point here is that the Law in Buddhist teaching is treated from first to last as immanent in human beings. Because the Law is immanent, its working in our lives depends on when and if we achieve self-awareness. The Buddha is sometimes called the Enlightened One, or the one with supreme self-awareness. And self-awareness is almost synonymous with autonomy.

For the Buddha, therefore, the one with supreme awareness, the truly painful question was whether or not it was possible for the countless, lost, ordinary people to attain self-awareness. Even if they could, would they be able to sustain it through the rough and tumble of human life? That is precisely why both Shakyamuni and Nichiren, after they had attained enlightenment, hesitated many times to teach the Law to the common people. They thought it might be an impossible mission. The inner realization of the Law has indeed been a major aporia throughout human history.

However, suppose that the Law were external to human beings; very quickly it would assume the nature of a heteronomous authority imposed on people, and the road to true autonomy would be closed. Many groups, religious or political, have, in fact, tried to impose systems from the outside and give them the force of law, and in so doing they have abused the authority they claimed to represent. As a result, people have been degraded to the level of slaves in the name of some law. The evidence is there before us in the bloody traces left by narrowly dogmatic and exclusive religious groups.

So it was wonderful for me to read the following passage by the great Spanish linguist Menéndez Pidal, depicting the internal norms of self-restraint and self-reliance – autonomy – that have given Spain's history its beautiful spirituality: 'The indomitable Spaniard, in his endurance against scarcity, holds in his bosom a level of wisdom that carries people through all manner of adversity; his standard is the call to "persevere and be temperate". Born with the spirit of Seneca, he has a basic, instinctive kind of stoicism within himself.'[8]

118

The second concept, symbiosis, speaks of living together in a mutually supportive relationship. In his meditation at the start of Goethe's play, Faust muses, 'How all things interweave as one / and work and live each in the other!'[9] Here he is struck by the vibrant symbiosis of everything in nature, awed at the way they interact, depend on each other, constantly moving in elaborate harmony. He feels his own alienation from the vast and generous expanse of life, which lets one breathe deeply and share one's own being with nature and the universe. Like Faust, modern people have been deeply estranged from the real fullness of life.

From the start, modern civilization has been underlain by an assumption that nature and humankind exist in opposition to each other; nature is an object to be conquered and controlled by human beings. It may be that human isolation and alienation have been the consequence of the demonic side of the Faustian ego.

As a great many thoughtful people have observed, it is urgent that this view of nature and the universe be revised if we wish to open a new horizon filled with promise for the next century. That is why the idea of symbiosis has increasingly come to symbolize hope for the future. I believe that Buddhism, with its unchanging promise of the unbreakable unity of humans and the environment – society, nature, the universe – offers the perfect vehicle to foster an all-embracing symbiosis.

To Live the Way of a Bodhisattva

Let us examine the principle known as *eshō-funi*. Very briefly, it encapsulates the idea of perfect symbiosis. *Eshō* is a combination of *shō-hō*, which means our own self, and *e-hō*, which means our environment, including nature. *Funi* literally means 'cannot be two', or unity. Together, then, *eshō-funi* signifies the inseparability of the two parts, life and its environment, that maintain a harmonious relationship as a single unit while interacting with and affecting each other. This is a fundamental principle of Buddhism. I hardly need add that it also represents a particular viewpoint that is rapidly becoming a major paradigm of postmodern epistemology.

In the Buddhist perspective, the harmony between humans and nature is not static. That harmony is an active, dynamic world throbbing with creative life. Its dynamism extends broadly enough to encompass all the active energy of the light, positive side of the modern ethos, that which should form its legacy for the new century: its spirit of progress, creativity, challenge, pioneering and so forth.

The dynamic relationship between *shō-hō* and *e-hō* is described by Nichiren as 'Without life, no environment. In the same way, life is shaped by its environment.'[10] The first part means that if you or I die, humankind will not cease to exist; rather, even if all humans were to become extinct, the universe would not come to an end. Nonetheless, as the second part tells us, in so far as the very existence of environment is contained within human beings, there can be no environment without life. This is less an objective representation than a statement of firm personal commitment based on self-evident religious truth, of the inseparability of humankind and nature.

The basis for subjective judgement is *ichinen*, or firm belief in Buddhism. Thus to say that *shō-hō* cannot exist without *e-hō* suggests that *ichinen* must extend to that boundless, vast expanse of the Greater Self that fills the universe, uncontained by any limits of time or space. The condition for *ichinen* is that we live by the teaching of the Greater Self, as opposed to the standards of the Lesser Self, or ego. Particularly in Mahayana Buddhism, we are called to live that way of life in compliance with the way of the Bodhisattva.

Subjective judgement has to be made very carefully, however, for without adequate ground, it can become the root of dogmatism or free-floating spiritualism, or even Faustian self-conceit. The second part of the teaching, 'even though life is supported by its environment', declares the impossibility of such a development by positing a balance between life and its environment, inserting what is basically the ecological idea of symbiosis. In that sense, the idea of *eshō-funi* presents itself as supremely modern. With appreciation of the environment, we are able to read into the somewhat inflexible proposition that 'Without life, environment cannot exist,' and see how it becomes a call for genuine symbiosis in which humans and the environment are intertwined in a dynamic mutual relationship that acts upon both equally.

One can hardly help noticing a remarkable parallel between *eshō-funi* and one of Ortega y Gasset's most powerful ideas: in effect, that I am simultaneously myself and my environment; if I cannot save my environment, I cannot save myself.[11] This thought implies elevation and expansion from ego to Greater Self, as in 'Without life, environment cannot exist.' And the second part of Ortega's statement is uncannily similar to 'Life is supported by its environment.' They both suggest a vector to symbiosis.

Listen to Ortega: 'Above all, civilization is the will to coexist.'[12] And hear the words of the philosopher Miguel de Unamuno: 'The strong person, the one who is primordially strong, can never be an egoist. A person with great power shares that power with others.'[13] Each in his own way is sharing with us his insight into part of an ethos of symbiosis, a cosmopolitan ethos that has navigated the spiritual ocean of Spain's history for several centuries since the age of exploration began. This symbiotic, cosmopolitan ethos finds deep resonance in the Bodhisattva way, the essence of Mahayana Buddhism.

My third topic is inner cultivation, which includes character building, discipline and training. I want to go into this because I believe modern civilization has squandered this value, leaving a serious gap. For the several hundred years since its emergence, our civilization has been running full tilt towards material benefits, convenience, comfort and efficiency. This created an unprecedented accumulation of wealth, which – at least materially – made it possible for ordinary people in industrial societies to live better than even the nobility of former times. But there have been high costs to pay in the form of severe social and other problems. The most serious ones are sometimes called the 'trilemma', a set of problems that plague every industrial country. Together they make up an interlocking structure of three major issues that operate on and exacerbate each other:

(1) economic development for ever-growing populations;
(2) exhaustion of natural resources and energy; and
(3) destruction of the environment.

I would say that an even more dangerous consequence of the advance of industrial civilization is the erosion of vitality and deterioration of people's inner world. In modern times, especially in the twentieth century, the tendency to latch onto the values of material gain and ever-increasing comfort has created a mindset that rationalizes easy solutions, shortcuts and superficiality, and unwisely neglects the importance of inner training. In a way, the former socialist countries seem to be suffering more than others for having put character building on a back burner.

Former USSR president Mikhail Gorbachev and I are currently conducting a dialogue for a leading Japanese opinion journal. In the course of our conversations he often comes back to this issue, speaking of the pitfalls of radicalism. For example, 'Like the temptation to make decisions in the simplest possible way, radicalism is stubborn. And how much hardship have people borne because of rushed decisions or the easy assumption that somehow a mysterious solution will appear and will take care of all the troubles at once.' In the same vein, he takes apart some favourite old notions: 'The nineteenth- and twentieth-century conviction that the most radical, the most revolutionary acts guarantee the endurance of change and progress was false.'[14]

Having critically observed the French Revolution, Goethe warned, 'Anything that simply liberates the spirit without affording a process of inner training is harmful.' That process of inner training is the cultivation of one's inner world. At different times and with different nuances others have expressed similar fears of institutional reforms that take place before people have undergone spiritual training and discipline. Some examples are the British philosopher Edmund Burke writing on the French Revolution; the French social historian Alexis de Tocqueville on the American Revolution; Mahatma Gandhi, concerned about the Russian Revolution; and Sun Yat-sen on China's 1912 revolution.

History has proven that their fears were not groundless. Now, at the end of this century, socialist and free societies alike are drenched in materialism and suffering from a fixation on wealth, and the collapse of morality. The age of the 'spoiled brat'[15] that Ortega described more than sixty years ago seems to have materialized today.

Human Revolution is Character Training

The traditional mode of character training centres on fortitude and endurance. Shakyamuni's last words were, 'Do not fail to complete your training.' Training of the inner person has always been a primary task in the Buddhist way of life.

Many of Nichiren's pronouncements speak directly to this theme: 'Iron, when heated in the flames and pounded, becomes a fine sword.'[16] 'Even a tarnished mirror will shine like a jewel if it is polished. A mind that is presently clouded by illusions originating from the innate darkness of life is like a tarnished mirror, but once it is polished, it will become clear, reflecting the enlightenment of immutable truth. Have deep faith and polish your mirror night and day.'[17] And, 'But still I am not discouraged. The Lotus Sutra is like the seed, the Buddha is like the sower, and the people are like the field.'[18]

You should note that each of these recommendations on how to refine one's inner self is framed in terms of a simile using concrete things – sword, mirror and planting fields. The world of farming and manual labour is distinct from other worlds, such as that of the printed word. To grow crops and perform work successfully with one's hands allows no skimping on labour, no shortcuts or easy substitutes for arduous procedures. Growing rice, for example, involves as many as eighty-eight steps until the harvest is in and stored. To omit any of them could bring less than satisfactory results. The same is true of tempering a high-quality sword or polishing a mirror. We can think of cultivating character and discipline, one's inner world, with just the same kind of logic. It is a demanding process that permits no omissions or shortcuts.

Nonetheless, the 'spoiled brats' produced by modern civilization turned their backs on the wise imperative of inner cultivation. So eager to live comfortable lives, always to choose the path of least resistance or rush to get quick results, they sometimes seem to be a different species, humans whose lives are played out in total indifference to what Ortega described as the 'Herculean tasks' that fall to people with rich, disciplined inner worlds.[19]

So it is that both the former socialist countries and the countries of the free world, the ostensible winners in the old battle of ideologies, have drifted into a thoughtless age of no philosophy except cynicism and mammonism. Somewhere in the deep layers of human beings and their history, I am certain that there is a conjunction between the untrained, undisciplined, flabby inner world of modern people and the mind-numbing, genocidal horror this century has witnessed. It is for this reason that we at Soka Gakkai are so adamant about the importance of human revolution, for it is another name for inner cultivation. We sail an uncharted course towards the dawn of a new century of humanity.

To recapitulate, I have put before you three major themes that promise to be crucial if we are to make the twenty-first century light and positive. They are autonomy, symbiosis and inner cultivation. Only history will be able to judge whether these qualities offered a beam of hope to the Faustian agony of purgatory. Whatever happens, no step can be taken without making the first step. To me, as one Buddhist devotee and a man of these times born to endure the trials of history, there is no choice but to work together with everyone else committed to the same objectives, doing all I can to help with the unprecedented task ahead.

I will close with a passage from *Don Quixote* that captures some of the spiritual quality of Spain and the Spanish people.

> A pilgrim knight should go into every corner of the world; enter into every difficult maze; bravely challenge the impossible, step by step; endure the burning summer heat of the desolate wild and endure the harsh cold of wind and snow in winter.[20]

APPENDIX 2

Sustainable Development Theory and National Development Strategy

Address by Dr Ricardo Díez-Hochleitner, Honorary President of The Club of Rome, to the Twenty-First-Century Forum, 'Sustainable Development: China and the World', Beijing, 5–8 September 2005

Summary

This occasion is an exceptionally good opportunity to deepen our dialogue between East and West. Face to face and hand in hand, we ought to discuss future strategies for sustainable development of China and the world, in a global approach, in spite of being faced with a world filled with uncertainties and in need of much more wisdom, solidarity and leadership.

To start with, we need to know much more and much better about this extraordinary country [China], together with facts about your achievements as well as problems you have yet to solve, in order to learn from you and to cooperate, if you so wish, using our global, interdisciplinary and long-term approach. To this end, a frank and honest inter-cultural dialogue is one of the most urgent needs in our common search for a global sustainable development in a more equitable world.

My dear friends,

Much has changed since the days of the birth of the Club of Rome, when it was rare to study and debate the world *problematique* on a long-term basis, transcending the borders of sovereign states, relating economic development to available natural resources and energy for the first time in an interdisciplinary long-term approach, such as has been the case in reports to the Club of Rome like *The Limits to Growth, The Chasm Ahead* and so on. Meanwhile, the ideas of complexity, interdependence and uncertainty have been widely extended, at least by words if not by deeds. Our task and renewed vocation is to be carriers of hope for the future, particularly when, in the face of such serious developmental and environmental problems as the ones threatening us nowadays, we become partners in our commitment to contribute to a reversal of the present most dangerous trends.

A quick retrospective look over the history of humanity shows a rising line that traces the undeniably immense material and cultural achievements made over a long and difficult march through millennia, particularly in the case of China. However, it also shows how often historical trends around the world have been seriously crippled by the ignorance and selfishness of too many, in particular of the wealthiest.

Today as never before, a vision of the future must be inspired by solidarity based on knowledge and ethical values, overcoming the widespread schematic, simplistic vision of a world divided between 'us – good guys' and 'them – bad guys'. Such thinking only hides our own private interests, fanaticisms and prejudices of all types. That is why it is now urgent to create feedback by means of debate among the great cultures and regions of the world.

In the final analysis, this paradoxical situation – that of a world burdened by setbacks and menaces yet crowned with extraordinary achievements and opportunities – suffers mainly from a lack of political, cultural and moral leadership or, more simply, a lack of a broader outlook. It seems as if we are being led only by the dictates of past experience, for a reality which no longer exists, instead of trying to build the future with renewed enthusiasm in the present millennium. Major political and economic powers will require profound restructuring (at least in the West) in order to make cooperation possible among all countries.

The principle of convergence, combined with flexibility, is a kind of cooperation that runs against centripetal trends, while supporting and developing cultural identities within each state as well as within and among regional communities, instead of creating protectionist blocs. Such a principle is even more valid and urgent in view of the indiscriminate, out-of-control territorial scope of environmental effects, in addition to the urgent need for subsequent sustainable development. Moreover, sustainable development requires a radical, completely comprehensive approach and mechanisms vested with universal authority. In fact, under present circumstances, no country nor any regional community can or should try to achieve sustainable development in isolation from the broader world context. To be viable, a more equitable world order requires the adoption of the principle of world cohesion as soon as possible through partnership, providing adequate compensations for less favoured countries, within the realm of a profoundly renewed United Nations.

It would be totally unacceptable and a serious setback to use present economic, financial and trade difficulties as an excuse to trample the currently timid feelings of human solidarity and the growing respect for human rights, hard-won in the aftermath of the last world war. Thus, simple monetary transfers or transfers in kind – including information and technology – are not enough; an overall approach of sustainable development is needed, inspired by solidarity as well as by long-term self-interest. In this spirit, businessmen must also assume a new leadership, not satisfied with just creating material well-being through legitimate profits but aiming at long-term, sustainable, viable business. This implies a new spirit of partnership (a new alliance) between the public and private sector in every field to serve the future of humankind better.

We in the Club of Rome are obliged to provide answers at this difficult turning point in history in order to contribute to the promotion of a new lifestyle. The new lifestyle should serve to overthrow the present economy of consumerism and waste, and enable sustainable development to satisfy the needs and aspirations of humanity, while protecting the environment and ensuring viable and enjoyable goals for future generations. To this end, economists, environmentalists and sociologists are urgently required to harmonize their views, to take fully into account the increasingly limited ecological options without jeopardizing progress within a genuine 'eco-socio-economy'.

However, in this perspective, present approaches continue to be superficial and wilful. Moreover, we are acting essentially in response to the symptoms of causes that have yet to be diagnosed, reacting as soon as we perceive events and menaces instead of attacking the root of long-term problems. Consequently, this 'Twenty-First-Century Forum: China' offers a unique and most timely opportunity to move ahead, in close partnership with the people of the whole world, towards a much better, viable and sustainable future.

The world is not condemned to death, but it is seriously sick, particularly as a result of the sick minds of many. It is therefore in their and our minds that we have to bring about a more equitable world based on sustainable development. The human brain is the most beautiful, most complex creation in the world, where knowledge, beliefs, conscience, creativity and individual inviolable sovereignty reside. This is the place where ideas are born, as well as the impulse behind our honest will and positive actions. It is because of this common human quality that the planet has cohesion and a promising future, since ideas based on ethical and moral values are in the end more powerful than any other factor in our universe. Such ideas, transformed into culture, are in turn indispensable for scientific and technological innovation, for inspiring economic, social and human sustainable development, and for political leadership. China has a unique opportunity for itself, as well as for the world at large to provide a most needed and effective leadership to resolve these vital issues.

The Background

The biosphere is humanity's habitat, and as such we must defend it and get to know it thoroughly. This real-life house for everyone, in which our most immediate surroundings are the Earth's crust and atmosphere, is also our one and only common heritage and, along with our cultural heritage and education, the only legacy we are required to leave to our descendants.

Our ability to improve our natural heritage is conditioned by many factors (assuming that we are motivated by global ethics and political intentions to do so), and in any case it is limited to nature. On the other hand, the biosphere's vulnerability is considerable, given mankind's enormous power to damage it rapidly and seriously, by commission and omission, and even to destroy it. However, preserving the biosphere means saving life, that is, first of all, ensuring survival, and in time, allowing us all to live decently in plenty.

Mankind has to accept the fact that available resources and the burden the ecosystem can bear are limited, and we must take into account the needs of future generations, who will rapidly grow in number. In spite of the extremely low population growth of many industrialized countries, overall world growth is now exponential. From about 500 million inhabitants in the year 1700 and 1.8 billion in 1900, we have gone to 4 billion in 1950, more than 6 billion in 2000 and probably around 9 billion in 2050. With lengthening life expectancy and the hoped-for decrease in infant mortality, the basic demands (food, housing, education and health) are constantly on the rise, but so is unbounded consumption in a society that very often identifies self with what one possesses instead of what one is and what one knows. That is why the impact of human activity on the biosphere has multiplied by a factor of 40 in the last century, and the world now produces in fifteen days what would have taken an entire year in 1900. Furthermore, the yawning disparities in technology and well-being between rich countries and poor countries are causing the current incipient massive migratory movements of the economic exiles of the future.

Therefore, while development does make for economic and social prosperity, what is most vital now is to preserve nature, to ensure that the earth can both support mankind's lasting development and maintain all the diverse expressions of life. Thus, nature conservation cannot be limited to specific, isolated action, praiseworthy though it may be, but requires a worldwide perspective and reach coming from the most varied of sectors, and must take into account the very different factors involved in order for our solutions to work. What it all boils down to is that nature conservation, and hence biosphere conservation, mean trying to solve the world's problems as a whole.

Our times are characterized on one hand by this worldwide spreading of action and the resulting worldwide assumption of responsibilities, which requires the adoption of global strategies. On the other hand, mankind has an almost unlimited capacity for creating and building to satisfy its needs and ambitions. In this process, we tend to use up natural resources without thinking about their scarcity in the future. The price nature pays for our ability for simultaneous destruction and spoliation is enormous. The list of dangers and disasters goes on and on: soil erosion, desertification, the disappearance of arable land, pollution, deforestation, damage and destruction to ecosystems, the extinction of species and biodiversity, polluted drinking water and oceans, ozone layer destruction, pollution of the atmosphere with nitrous and sulphurous gases and carbon dioxide, with the resulting greenhouse effect, climate change and so on.

More than thirty years ago, the Club of Rome scandalized the world with a report prepared by an MIT team at our request in order to verify whether unlimited economic development had a future or whether there were limits to growth. As soon as the effects of the 1973 oil crisis had settled, the more industrialized countries went back to behaving like happy-go-lucky, confident cities which, while proclaiming the end of linear economic growth, continued with their wasteful economy and pro-consumption culture. Their prime objective was maximum annual gross national product growth, as if there were no limits to the available natural resources or the wealth that could be accumulated by a few industrialized countries. Now, three decades later, with the world standing at a crossroads, while the market economy (though a mere economic tool if not synonymous with human, social and cultural development) is advocated as the universal golden calf, the world may already be observed to have overstepped, probably irreversibly, some of the most sacred boundaries of nature, including the extinction of plant and animal species, air, water and land pollution, and an alarming pillaging of all kinds of resources that are necessary to provide for the needs of the human population.

Biodiversity is vitally important for mankind for many reasons, and yet it is increasingly threatened by the current rapid extinction of animal and plant species. Its importance is as much economic (since it is the source of food, clothing, medicines, housing and resources such as tourism) as it is scientific (for the protection and conservation of farmable land, weather regulation and photosynthesis). In addition, it has other values, intangible, aesthetic ones that inspire artists. For all these reasons, many of us are convinced that the diversity of life contributes significantly to the quality of life, and that thus we have a moral obligation to protect biodiversity as a precious bequest of life itself for our successors.

No single one of the many serious environmental phenomena now known or the many new ones that may surprise us in the near future is necessarily more important than the rest. In fact, the atmosphere is being polluted by industrial detritus that falls back to earth in the form of acid rain; by toxic gases (especially nitric and sulphurous gases); by organic gases given off by swamps, livestock and human beings (methane); and cooling industry products such as HFCs (hydrofluorocarbons), etc. Nevertheless, one of the most serious phenomena we know of – the result of interaction between industry, urban development and the environment – is the carbon dioxide given off into the atmosphere along with other polluting gases, due mainly to the combustion of coal and hydrocarbons. The more than 0.5 per cent annual net increase in the concentration of carbon dioxide in the atmosphere (about 3,500 metric megatons) is due to the fact that mankind has forced things beyond the world's ability to balance the ecology.

The resulting greenhouse effect (the debate on which was opened by Arrhenius at the beginning of the last century) can now be noticed everywhere, and it threatens to change our air and water temperature gradients in less than fifty years, with dramatic effects on the polar regions. A conservative estimate is that the average temperature will have risen by more than four degrees before the end of this century. So then, saving the world's forests, which help absorb carbon dioxide through photosynthesis, is a very important step in the right direction. However, an extraordinary amount of absorption used to be done by the oceans in their interaction with the atmosphere, thanks to marine life (plankton, etc.) and deep-sea clays, until a creeping, generally invisible, film produced by all kinds of liquid waste dumping formed a surface barrier. We can only hope that research now under way will show how serious the problem is, so that perhaps political and economic interests will unfreeze and an effective world solution can be found.

Along these lines, we must also remember that the constantly expanding holes in the ozone layer are not to be feared only because of the skin cancer and cataracts they cause in people and animals, but also because today's excessive concentration of ultraviolet rays in increasingly large regions of the planet effect people, animals and plant species, including sea plankton, by destroying, among other things, the structure of albumins and the DNA molecule, as well as causing a gradual deterioration of immunological defences. All this exacerbates the proliferation of diseases such as hepatitis, herpes, malaria and AIDS, just to mention a few, with the serious risk of generating pandemic illness. Even more frightening is the possibility that it may favour the mutation of some of the vast number of viruses present in the human organism that are as yet innocuous.

We must also become aware of the steadily growing scarcity of accessible drinking water, which is due not only to increasing human consumption but also to agricultural overuse and irrigation using wasteful techniques on the surface (sprinklers), as well as the progressive contamination of aquifer reserves. That is why it is urgent for us to upgrade considerably our efficiency in using available water, and to try and prevail over the terrible pandemic disease and famine that hold many needy countries in their merciless grip today. However, for the record, today mankind barely consumes 0.001 per cent (3,500km³ a year) of the total available drinking water, and all that needs to be done is to change the current priorities of technological research, which could surely find economical solutions and increase the practical availability of drinking water for consumption and for a more rationalized agriculture than we currently use.

We must not forget that the oceans cover close to 70 per cent of our planet's surface. In spite of this, the oceans, or at least their morphology, continue to be a big scientific unknown. The physical, chemical, biological and other processes and the circulating currents of the oceans are still marginalized in environmental research, in spite of their decisive importance (for instance in the greenhouse effect, as indicated above). The more than 6.5 million tons of waste that end up each year in the sea and rivers and the non-biodegradable synthetic material and mercury compounds thrown into the oceans considerably worsen world water pollution.

The impact of human activity may be seen everywhere and, of course, in the spoiling and contamination of the earth itself as well, which has been considerably influenced by the last four decades' settlement trends. Nowadays close to half the population (around 3 billion inhabitants) live inside a strip of coastline no more than sixty kilometres wide, so coastal research is urgent if we are to attend to the needs of the populations residing there and at the same time protect coastal ecosystems.

The entire Earth is under merciless, progressively worsening attack because of man's action (for instance, the destruction of twenty hectares of tropical rainforests per minute, or the acid rain caused by industry, which speedily destroys forests and systematically makes the organic layer of farmable land sterile). To counteract this, fertilizers (especially nitrates, which increased from 60,000 metric tonnes in 1970 to 140,000 in 1990) are used to increase farming output, but in this case the danger is from filtration – by which the chemicals used may wind up reaching the water held in aquifer reserves, even in watertight aquifers – and from other pollutants in herbicides and pesticides, which also jeopardize biodiversity.

These polluting effects, which form an endless list – of which I have very briefly mentioned only a few – interact with each other in turn with still unpredictable results, quite apart from the dramatic effects of many natural catastrophes (earthquakes, volcanoes, landslides and cyclones), which have increased dramatically in number and importance (such as the recent tsunami) and have cost the lives of millions of victims.

In spite of the problems that have accumulated over recent decades, our planet has gradually filled with people, little by little at first and spectacularly of late, while our desire for well-being is reaching levels of consumption never before imaginable, even by the richest, in humanity's long, grand, often painful path towards a civilization of the universal in search of greater quality of life in all regards – though the final result may be just the opposite. The ups and downs of progress are a long list of conquests and failures, problems and achievements, challenges and opportunities, in which hope cannot, must not, die out. However, if we relate the world's widespread insatiable consumption with accelerated population growth, we can see that the impact of human activity on the biosphere in the last century has multiplied by forty, with a world product of about $20 trillion. If every country in the world consumed as much as the most industrialized countries, about 200 times more mineral resources and about ten times more fuel resources would be required.

In spite of this, the disparities in well-being splitting the world in two are immense and growing; the industrialized part of the world has access to 75 per cent of the world's product with barely 15 per cent of the total population, while the rest live in ignorance, illness and hunger, at the mercy of the elements. Many of them even reside in the heart of the greatest emporia of wealth. The USA, with 5 per cent of the world's population, produces 25 per cent of the total GNP (while it spends 25 per cent of the world's energy and emits 22 per cent of the total carbon dioxide). The cases of dramatic imbalance abound throughout the world, for example, between the OECD countries and Africa, East and West Europe, North and South America, etc. Poverty thus may be seen as the world's worst 'pollution'. That is why it is not odd that we start to see growing social confrontations within many countries now – and imminent great migratory movements of economic exiles if we do not help put an end to underdevelopment locally and reduce existing demographic trends – and uncompromising fanatic rejection of all modernization in favour of austerity.

In the face of these new realities, which can range beyond the imaginings of science fiction, our view of the world and the shape of things need to change radically. Thus it may come to be that the greatest threat to survival may cease to be the use of atomic bombs in a worldwide conflagration (all the more so since we are now living in an era of relative truce between the superpowers) or the establishment of tyrannies run by brutal powers, to be replaced by the overlapping, relatively slow global catastrophe of the destruction of the biosphere that sustains us.

Along with these considerable problems, there are, fortunately, numerous positive aspects that play a part in the broad panorama of the world's problems to meet these and other challenges. At least there is increasing awareness of the interdependence of countries and the spreading of environmental phenomena around the globe. This very forum is an excellent example for a new global trend. Though there is still some resistance, the more industrialized countries are beginning to accept a certain global environmental responsibility as well as their responsibilities within their own borders, and the less developed countries are increasingly recognizing the threat that their poor management and the resulting damage to their own environmental heritage represent for them in the medium term if they are to achieve greater well-being. In turn, the Eastern countries are seriously concerned about the environmental impact of their high-pollution industrial processes.

Moreover, new technologies and new materials are inspiring great hope, especially since they are beginning to be valued in terms of their impact on the environment; and technologies for increasing the efficiency of energy resources, natural resources and pollution control are spreading systematically. What is more, the outlooks for having fusion energy (although not before 2050) have improved lately, which would mean abundant, relatively clean, cheap energy.

Furthermore, of even greater importance is the progressive (though still totally insufficient) advance in national and international law regulating ecological crimes; environment-oriented institutional development for research, control, technological transfer, financial compensations and swapping; and the promotion of environmental development policies in order to ensure a development that is economically, socially and humanly sustainable. To this end, the introduction and expansion of environmental education programmes in educational systems and non-formal teaching is fortunately starting to come under consideration.

Anyway, many measures must be taken as soon as possible, starting by establishing a full world inventory of the natural heritage currently available and the polluting, desolating processes currently operating in nature as a whole on land, at sea and in the air, in addition to the progressive interaction of these negative effects, which cannot be encompassed by any partial view. In any case, environmental development policies must be promoted, and an effort must be made to reconcile economic and ecological language and concepts and to adopt environmental defence and nature conservation legislation inspired by principles of international cooperation.

To sum up: access to knowledge about the current state of and future outlooks for the evolution of the biosphere and learning about viable present and future measures for effective nature conservation and sustainable development are a duty and a right of the utmost priority and importance for us all. The current suicidal confrontation between man and nature must be transformed as soon as possible into a harmonious relationship.

The Theory

The United Nations Conference on the Environment and Development in Rio de Janeiro in June 1992 was organized around the most fundamental topic the world community has to deal nowadays: how to reconcile human activity conducive to economic and social development with the laws of nature. In many ways, the Earth Summit was a failure, and in any case it was a big disappointment for the hopes that the more optimistic of us held, though the mere fact that it was held at all was a positive surprise. The Declaration of Rio reflects at least the degree of consensus at that time in point on a set of action-inspiring principles, though it did fall very short of the initially foreseen Earth Charter. The Accords on Climatic Change and Biodiversity had little punch, since they set no specific objectives or deadlines and because of the United States' reticence and absence at signing. Thus, Agenda 21 continues to run the risk of becoming a worthless piece of paper without enough financial commitments: $625 billion per year were estimated necessary in order to apply the objectives of Agenda 21 fully; the increase in funds for the Global Environment Facility (GEF) with $1.3 billion, was to be administered by the World Bank in cooperation with UNDP and UNEP, in addition to the relatively substantial promises made by Japan towards an increase of about $4 billion until 1997, and Germany dedicating 0.7 per cent of its GNP to technical cooperation for 'sustainable development', as a suggested goal for industrialized countries. However, little progress has taken place till now. Nevertheless, the most important leap forward in quality was the conference's adoption of the principle and goal of sustainable development as being indissolubly linked to humankind and environmental protection, though the concept and scope of sustainable development was not clearly enough defined nor its viability clearly established.

The idea and theory of sustainable development did spread little by little from around 1969, when it became obvious that linear economic growth, almost unchallenged until then (*The Chasm Ahead*, Aurelio Peccei), was not viable in the long run. The report drawn up in 1972 by the MIT team (*The Limits to Growth*) at the request of the Club of Rome and the report later, in 1987, by the United Nations World Committee on the Environment and Development (*Our Common Future*), presided over by Ms Bruntland, contributed decisively to this new language. However, looking back since the late 1960s and in spite of the supposed new goals of economic, social and human development as opposed to just linear economic growth, Western economies and the economies of developing countries continued holding obsessively to the linear growth as their basic model. Therefore, the danger before us now lies in turning sustainable development into a myth and continuing to mask linear economic growth with new expressions of good will.

Thus, the hard part now is to establish the right definition of sustainable development and the corresponding indispensable national development strategy for its practical application. Moreover, we need to succeed in mobilizing the political will of all governments together with an active democratic participation by all citizens of the world.

Sustainable development promotes and attains the greatest material and social well-being for all, in tune with the specific aspirations of each cultural identity, while acknowledging its serious duty not to endanger similar aspirations by future generations to inhabit our planet. However, in order for us to reach this goal, praiseworthy strategies for sustainable development in local areas, national areas or even regions such as Europe, North America or China – although most desirable and necessary – are not enough separately. On the contrary, sustainable development as defined above requires a global strategy, a shared framework and, as a result, mechanisms or institutions wielding universal authority, in order to avoid any excess, abuse or imbalance in the use of natural resources, pollution from industrial and agricultural production, the unorganized manipulation of trade and international finances, etc. We must take into account the fact that, considered individually, countries are units with their own very different quantities and types of natural and human resources. Furthermore, each has reached a level of development very different from the rest in the course of its own history. That is why sustainable world development also requires that we start by taking worldwide stock of existing human and natural resources, planetary pollution, all current industrialization and agricultural development, in addition to other items, in order to establish global strategies, goals and limits as well as mutual compensation quotas, within whose parameters each country should then act.

National Development Strategy

The only way for us to make up our minds to change the current socioeconomic system is to admit that it cannot be maintained and that, if we continue as at present, then we are heading for collapse. Obviously, each society hopes to ensure its own survival above all and also to attain the highest quality of life. The task consists of allowing all societies and regions of the world, the entire world, to satisfy similar hopes, to start with, without any one being worse off than any other, and without endangering the needs and expectations of tomorrow's inhabitants of that zone, country or region of the planet.

The goal of sustainable development starts with the current situation, in which it turns out that we have already trespassed beyond various limits that we should have set for ourselves years ago, particularly in pollution and the wasting of resources. But in this attempt, one most important factor is a balanced distribution of the population throughout territories, in order to make possible a suitable sustainable quality of life for the number of inhabitants covering each area. On this point, I would like to say that today, like yesterday and tomorrow, demographic evolution should always be the product of the freedom of individual consciences and education, within principles of solidarity, and we should avoid manipulating life with Malthusian or procreation policies serving economic interests. That is why it is vital in our first focus on the problem to establish a rational relationship between each human group and the natural system sustaining it (what is called the system's capacity).

Furthermore, sustainable development can be attained only if we modify the dominant lifestyle and our current messy, pro-consumption habits, and admit that the lifestyle parameters that are currently most widespread are unsustainable and are not those of a quality of life that deserves to be defended. This will mean a far-reaching metamorphosis of the current system, a great transition similar to the one that occurred between the agricultural revolution and the industrial revolution, in which we must make an affirmation of mankind, not industrialization at all costs.

In this spirit, economic and ecological concepts must be reconciled as soon as possible until we can admit fully that damage to the environment represents a loss of capital stock, a loss of the natural heritage of each state, as well as involving a heavy social cost. All of this must be taken into account upon setting and collecting the prices of goods and services and must be reflected in national accounting. For all these reasons it is also essential that we raise systematic opposition to hiding, withholding and manipulating available data on resource use and air, water and territorial pollution.

From all this there can and must arise the guarantee of an green socioeconomy and a quality of life that, at a suitable level of generalized material welfare, not only covers basic essential needs but also monitors fairness, accepts existing physical limits, recognizes human limits (institutional limits and the limits of cultural identities and social models) and encourages suitable consumption of recyclable products, shunning all obsessive consumption for consumption's sake.

It is the young who are the best placed at this early stage of the twenty-first century to allow the dawn of this new society that assumes its duties and its rights with wisdom and solidarity. This means wisdom, as opposed to genuine or self-interested ignorance; respect for history and the essential values, as opposed to contra-cultural materialism; research, creativity and innovation, as opposed to laziness and individual or group pessimism; solidarity, as opposed to short-sighted, pro-consumption selfishness; individual liberty, as opposed to aping old obsolete models; responsible individual participation in democracy, as opposed to opportunist sector-oriented demagogies; peace among nations and peace between mankind and the biosphere, as opposed to fratricidal or suicidal violence and confrontation.

A new business leadership is also indispensable. We need leaders who will create wealth with private initiative and, while managing their exactable, legitimate profits with clear income statements, will not fail to add in political action with equally global, long-term focuses, for the sake of their own work. In this regard, private enterprise management has no choice but to change its paradigm to reach far beyond its business impact on its immediate surroundings, with social, cultural, ecological and global ethical direction. Corporate social responsibility, together with innovations against their respective air, earth and water pollution level, is not only an ethical must but is moreover the indispensable condition for any enterprise to become sustainable.

In this respect, the doctrine of the market economy, fashionable as it still is nowadays, obviously contributes to short-term economic development and industrial innovation, but the indiscriminate application of its mechanisms not only fails to solve the serious human, social and environmental problems that concern us all, but it worsens them, unless combined with research and technological innovation as well as with a very broad view and a long-term strategy in order to deal with the vast interdependence and current complexity of any sector. Thus, reaffirmations that linear consumption and demand have their limits should come as no surprise. What is more, the concept of indefinite economic growth is plainly and simply an aberration unless e.g. world population is not distributed according to the capacity of each settlement, or the production of fusion energy soon finds an industrial solution, etc. In the meantime, market economy and everything else that does not strive towards real sustainable development implies contempt for the majority of peoples and persons for the benefit of a few, especially since today economic growth means proportionally multiplying energy and material resource requirements, along with increasingly well-known environmental and, more specifically, climate change and health repercussions, among others. This is something that the People's Republic of China has to consider very seriously at its present most important juncture of a potential explosive development, with all its opportunities and challenges. China could and should become a world leader, not only in providing practical guidance for national development strategies around the world, but particularly in its own short- and medium-term interest.

The United Nations Development Programme (UNDP) has already correctly pointed out that the predictable 'clamour for sustainable development is not just a call for environmental protection, for it also implies a new concept of economic growth providing justice and opportunities for all people of the world instead of the privileged few, without destroying the world's finite natural resources any further or hazarding the Earth's carrying capacity.'

However, despite its undoubted positive contributions, goals such as those adopted by the Protocol in Kyoto were not as conclusive as they should have been. Shadows overcast many aspects of the conference debates, which were approached from the too-often selfish positions of the representatives of nation states whose analyses of global-scale problems were considerably partial. Along with defensive presentations of their own actions, they essentially limited themselves to formulating solutions from their own sovereignties' perspectives, and selfishness prevailed, as it did in contributions of resources and work towards finding a global solution. As a result, it is mainly topics native to each country's domestic environment that continue to be dealt with, such as forests and the biodiversity that is to be protected therein, and the action that each country can and should take to contribute to solving global-scale problems, such as the climatic shift. However, all matters concerning our common heritage (the global commons) were left dramatically unresolved since they lay outside the direct mandate of each state. These are matters such as the oceans and the biodiversity sheltered in them, the polar territories, the stratosphere, and the problem of the balanced growth of the world population and the prevention of future pandemics due to environmental causes, etc. Most disappointing remains the fact that the USA has not yet agreed to sign the Protocol and honour its goals and commitments.

Consequently, the notion of sustainable development remains utopian or not viable unless we introduce at least some stocktaking, a view, a strategy and some mechanisms for supranational action to add to the country-by-country strategies in order to take full stock of the overall real complexity. This is the indispensable starting point for any real endeavour with specific goals and suitable means, and it is vital in order to determine the tendency of human activity's negative environmental impact in the different regions of the world. Only based on these data can pollution emission quotas and mutually agreed compensations be established, within mechanisms wielding international authority, until we can make harmonious global sustainable development.

Jean Monnet said that, 'The sovereign countries of the past cannot ensure their own progress or control their own future,' so inexorably they have to fall back on dealing with supranational communities. But this is just the first phase, which requires that authority very soon be delegated on development issues of common concern to a new United Nations, renovated under international cooperation. In today's aberration, several elements of an international order are practically in the hands of the Group of Seven or Eight (G7/G8), or rather, in the hands of the superpower that won the Cold War, instead of a 'G 200' – a fully empowered and restructured United Nations Organization. The main recommendation of the 1992 Earth Summit was the creation of a high-level UN Committee on Sustainable Development. But even if constituted, its effectiveness would depend on its composition, working methods, authority and impact on public opinion.

An ethical basis is the key for lasting honest action. But ethics alone are not enough. Environmental topics must be depoliticized; the branch of environmental law must be established with far-reaching, encouraging, legislation; democratic terms of office must not be allowed to shape long-term goals and programmes. This focus does not depend only on the vision of politicians who want to get a jump on events, but mostly on leaders and citizens who should demand long-term solutions instead of short-term answers to satisfy our selfish aspirations to immediate well-being. In this perspective, anticipatory democracies are the next urgent step, assuming that participatory democracies are already in place. The media play a decisive role in this matter, so they bear a correlative responsibility; not only do they have to inform but they also should contribute to stimulating and motivating the public to seek out knowledge and participate in action on topics that are very often serious and painful.

The Rio de Janeiro Conference did not adopt an ethical code of individual and collective behaviour, as would have been necessary in order to inaugurate a new age of the affirmation of mankind instead of the culture of waste, wild consumption and selfishness. Nor was the Conference explicit on the priority of environmental education in all realms and at all levels of human learning, though this was in the minds of many and was the debating ground of one of the round tables to which I was invited. What was made clear to all was that the subject's verbiage quota had been met, and the time had come for massive action by all – poor and rich, countries and private initiatives alike – starting by making that vital change in everyone's lifestyle and instilling a new sensitivity towards the environment.

The Earth Summit was a big, positive, necessary step, but by no means enough to ensure the survival of the human species on a planet whose biosphere is being torn apart at a fast pace. It is to be hoped that from now on all countries will generate a powerful change, with effective measures and the participation by every country under growing international coordination.

As a result, the sovereign nation states are going to need supranational formulas in order to survive in a world that will become progressively interdependent in all fields. A new international order can and should arise from all countries in concert in the heart of the United Nations, an order independent of any hegemonic power. This new UN, which must be rather the Organization for the Union of the Nations (so often disunited!) or rather of the People, must succeed in involving itself, on behalf of all people and nations of the world, in the so-called 'internal affairs' of countries when they seriously affect human rights and the greater common good of both humanity and the biosphere.

Meanwhile, we are standing in the face of the need for a great human revolution of education and culture. We have to advance from the view of man as the conqueror and exploiter of nature to the view of man as the administrator of nature on viable, sustainable bases. But that entails not only intellectual and ethical aspects but also the reworking of the specific interests of power structures at all levels. The action that must be taken does not depend only on our knowledge but also on the power structure, political ideas and private interests. That is why it is essential to increase knowledge, education and effective public participation. We must try and create a new human awareness, an ethical structure for survival and sustainable progress, taking the best of the wisdom of all peoples and cultures of the world. This should reflect the rights of future generations and the rights of today's needy, the rights of all other living beings, affirming our respect for the biosphere that sustains us.

144

In our world there are basically two types of people: those who put up walls against cooperation and those who build bridges in favour of solidarity. Those who put up walls are the envious, the racist, the selfish, the haughty and those who cannot let go of their grudges or rancour. Such people are at the root of sadness, discrimination, poverty, violence and war.

The bridge builders are people of kindness (towards mankind and nature), forgiveness, tolerance, justice, sustainable development and peace. Without them our world would cease to exist.

Let us hope that we all, together, will succeed in building a better world.

Dr Ricardo Díez-Hochleitner
15 July 2005, Madrid

Concluding Remarks by Dr Ricardo Díez-Hochleitner at the Closing Session of the Twenty-First-Century Forum, on Behalf of Panel 4

Panel 4 on 'Effective and Wise Use of Natural Resources' dealt with these issues during two enriching morning sessions on 6 September 2005. The debates were kept very much in line with the spirit of mutual understanding, willingness to cooperate and in full awareness of the serious challenges as well as opportunities that exist around the world. Such has been also – in my view – the spirit that has presided constantly at the Twenty-First-Century Forum since its opening session.

Chinese leaders, government officials, intellectuals and experts, as well as foreign leaders and participants, have spoken freely and openly about the present and near-future growing problems, particularly in terms of the demands of both natural resources and energy required to overcome the dangers involved in future economic growth and consequent social crisis, within and among our countries, particularly between China and the rest of the world, in spite of its growing population and consequent grow-ing demands. Panel 4 did review the present situation and future trends of resources required and potential supply, both from the point of view of the Chinese high officials and experts, as well as seen by leading people from the Asian region – including the ASEAN countries, Japan and Australia – in addition to those from Western countries and those representing international organizations, e.g. UNESCO, UNDP, the European Union, Asian Bank, World Bank, etc.

However, the debate has shown that the West speaks different languages on policies, corresponding to the European Union, the USA and Latin America. Instead, solidarity and friendship on the part of the majority of people flows from an increasing conscience about our common future, given the global extent of the human impact, worldwide potential energy crisis, pollution, climate change and so on, which can be overcome only through global strategies and concerted local actions.

With the Twenty-First-Century Forum, China is taking a major step forward in the analysis of the most crucial problems and in reviewing alternative solutions, economic models and implementation strategies, for example, regarding population growth, urban development versus low rural levels, alternative energies and energy efficiency, etc.

Session 2 of Panel 4 has provided abundant, concrete and solid information about the present and prospective situation regarding agriculture, food, water supply, as well as about important domestic geological supplies and limitations (mainly mineral oil). On the other hand, outside observers have shown considerable alternative energy sources (e.g. solar and eolic energy or fusion energy in the long run) besides new development viable avenues that China may wish to choose and adopt, particularly by establishing partnership agreements and cooperative programmes with foreign corporations, governments or supranational, entities. In this perspective, updated education and training at all levels needs to be widespread and supported by all as a top priority.

China is not to be seen as the 'bad guy' or 'the menace' to anyone because of its great endogenous development and consequent growing needs. On the contrary, China deserves, now as never before, all the understanding, admiration and cooperation that can be offered in building a new world order in peace and with well-being to overcome major disparities, poverty and violence all over the world.

146

The relationships between China and most of the highly industrialized countries of the world are still beset with ambiguity. Too many are increasingly concerned with China´s rapidly expanding export trade and growing demand of mineral oil as well as of other natural resources, while forgetting that the most industrialized countries in the world consume right now more than 75 per cent of the world's total natural resources for the benefit of only about 15 per cent of the world population. Consequently, the rise of China, together with India and eventually Brazil, will soon bring about a substantial reordering of the international system, including the world trade flow of natural resources due to its global economic and financial growth. Europe, Latin America and the USA have to deal and cooperate as equal independent partners.

Fortunately, China has always shown a prudent approach in international affairs (in spite of having suffered colonialism before), exercising patience and careful study before action, coherent with its millenary culture and corresponding widespread wisdom.

What we all need to reach now, as soon as possible, is a partnership for a strategic development towards a globally acceptable new world order, intended to achieve the universal aspiration for peace, progress and sustainable development.

7 September 2005, Beijing

APPENDIX 3

Statement to the General Assembly of the World Academy of Art and Sciences

Statement by Dr Ricardo Díez-Hochleitner, honorary president of the Club of Rome to the General Assembly of the World Academy of Art and Sciences, Zagreb (Croatia) 19 November 2005

Dear President of the World Academy,

Dear colleagues; ladies and gentlemen,
   We all should aim at spreading education for peace in order to live in democratic harmony and freedom, besides achieving sustained and sustainable global development, inspired by ethical values consistently exercised throughout our lives.
   Violence exists, unfortunately, not only in times of great conflagration and crisis. Violence is and has always been a part of every society. Moreover, the conditions which are propitious to a culture of violence include poverty, ignorance and egoism, all of which are very much spread around the world.
   In times past, the powerful regarded conquest by way of war to be the shortest route to subsequent material progress for the

conquerors. And yet the lesson to be learned from history is that war has always been a vehicle for endless calamity, bringing much greater sacrifice and grief than could be offset by any possible material benefits. The conclusion is that democratic coexistence and peace are the safest way, the firmest ground, to promote new avenues of development. Indeed, true development will not be possible until peace prevails throughout the world.

Nevertheless, peace in the world continues to be precarious, all too often disrupted by the serious conflicts of varying nature and scope in which scores of countries around the world are involved. And at the same time, terrorist violence is spreading and threatening to upset the delicate balance of governance in many countries and, therefore, opposing the goal of worldwide peace.

Prejudice, discrimination, hatred, xenophobia, selfishness and deep-rooted cultural deformation underlie most conflicts and explain the absence or shortage of democratic harmony among the peoples of this planet. In any event, communities living in mutual respect – an essential requisite to peace – will not be effective or feasible in the long run if imposed by force without mutual solidarity, tolerance and justice. Endeavouring to come to know and understand others, beginning with their respective religious, cultural and political convictions, are the only way to be genuinely tolerant – or rather having respect for every human being – and to exercise the dialogue on which justice, cooperation and peace are founded. Otherwise, refusing to accept dialogue is tantamount to refusing to be human beings.

Active and generalized peace among all the world's inhabitants, based on constructive dialogue, is indispensable to the sustainable development needed to live in spiritual and material plenitude. Such is the precondition for well-being and happiness among all human beings, as well as for humankind and nature to live in harmony.

Indeed, peace is the best argument for the only battle that is worth being fought by each generation and each people: the battle for cultural, social and economic development or, in other words, for spiritual and material progress in freedom and justice.

Today's instability is usually explained in terms of geo-political 'reasons of State' (*la raison d'État*), but these reasons are often driven by an underlying ambition to attain ideological, economic and military domination, reinforced by national pride and deep incomprehension. Such lack of understanding thrives in the absence of a solid intercultural and inter-denominational dialogue such as that so intensely defended by the Club of Rome and needed to facilitate the sober analysis and correct interpretation of all available information. Add to this the materialistic selfishness and the economic and financial crisis, and thus it is no wonder that there is a lack of leadership truly committed to peace, a goal gratuitously proclaimed while at the same time sullied and belittled.

Shortly before his death, my unforgettable and much admired friend Aurelio Peccei, founder of the Club of Rome, wrote, 'To invent a better future is to invent a better manner of being to be able to survive and progress [. . .] Fundamental re-thinking is indispensable. Only a new kind of humanism can work this semi-miracle: provoking the rebirth of spiritual values in humanity, from the inside [. . .], in other words, a genuine human revolution.'

In short: the beginnings of this new century and millennium could well pave the way to a rebirth of humanism, the birth of a new era of generalized democratic coexistence and world peace. But in order to deal successfully with such an enormous challenge it is indispensable first to be fully aware of the scope of the present situation and the serious risks involved, and act as soon as possible with determination and vigour to mobilize the political will and creativity needed to attain the kind of development in peace pursued through effective peace education.

Ladies and gentlemen,

I wish still to insist that the world, in these early years of the third millennium, continues to be imbued with a feeling of insecurity and anxiety that cuts across the obvious areas of defence and law and order, terrorism and the forces struggling to attain hegemonic power, but also extends to the shameful and scandalous growth of extreme poverty in some countries and even whole continents. And this feeling is reinforced by economic and financial crises, technological 'bubbles', the severe and ever-speedier deterioration of the environment and the conflict between cultures and convictions. At the same time, the moral relativism prevailing in

151

our societies denotes a growing inconsistency between frequently heralded values and ideologies and actual attitudes towards all these problems and challenges.

Within the broad panorama of what the Club of Rome calls the 'world *problematique*', peace is certainly the most highly valued aim. However, it is hardly novel to note that defence or security is no longer limited to the military dimension per se, although this is also essential, because it must always be global in nature, encompassing civil defence, defence of the economy and defence of the environment, including the defence of the quality of food, water and health, always in the context of cooperation and consensus among the international community.

Ladies and gentlemen, dear colleagues,

We, the citizens of the world, are thus in need of a great human revolution not only to overcome all forms of violence, but also to curb material poverty as well as cultural and moral poverty, thanks to education, science and culture. Such a revolution, therefore, entails not only intellectual and moral aspects, but also the knowledge about specific interests in the structures of political and economic power at all levels. We must attempt to build a new human conscience; an ethical structure for survival and sustainable progress, drawing on the wisdom of all the world's peoples and cultures in order to educate in favour of democratic life in community.

However, without changes in society, education alone cannot resolve all causes of conflict. The strongest mind cannot vanquish the starving body. The best lessons in equality and respect cannot alone negate a culture of abuse. Education is, however, the most powerful means at our disposal to countermand the call to violence.

Education provides training for living and to overcome poverty. But education is fortunately much more than about dollars or euros: it is about values, about learning to live and about living for learning (lifelong learning). Education is the acquisition of knowledge and a social equalizer, thus also the *sine qua non* of participatory and anticipatory democracy. Montesquieu already signalled that tyranny flourishes where ignorance

152

thrives. Democracy, he wrote, requires an educated population. Education offers the means to establish a politics of participatory and anticipatory governance, as well as the means to eliminate repression and subjugation of all kinds.

Consequently, education is also a moral force. It is a way of teaching and learning tolerance and respect. Since the time of the Socratic dialogue, education is a social act which involves an exchange, not only of information but of ideas, concepts and values. Education is a privilege and therefore those who have access to it have to accept certain responsibilities. Education provides an understanding of one's own identity and must be accompanied by recognition of the needs of others. Finally, education is the discovery of truth and beauty which, once reached, becomes the motor and motivation for all the people.

In the Masai language the word for peace is the same as the word for beauty. The linkage of these two terms provides an important subliminal message. Without peace, there cannot be beauty. The words we use to describe any concept indicate our subconscious value system. For very many, weak and soft are not positive attributes, while powerful is seen as valid and valuable. We teach our children to prize the very attributes of bellicosity. Even truth and beauty are viewed with some discomfort. They are not scientifically measurable. They are individually perceived and their nobility is questioned with their very elusiveness. Too often, even poets and teachers are undervalued and viewed with some suspicion because of their language.

Since the Renaissance there have been admirable projects to create international languages. Even today Esperanto remains a gleam in some eyes. We do not need an international language to substitute for all others. We do not need to select a single global language: we already have an unsurmountable global one, such as written or played music. We just need to learn other languages in order to gain sensitivity and better understand other cultures. In fact, we mainly need to pay attention to the words we choose and use in any language, since the pen is indeed mightier than the sword. Thus, let us put the pen to serve the cause of peace.

On another line, we see nowadays everything as compartmentalized. This affects the way we think and is often responsible for the violent reaction of the local at almost every intersection with the global. This fragmented way of thinking impacts on the way we see the world. We bravely talk of the global but we cannot truly think globally. For example, we used to talk about globalizing the curriculum. By this we usually mean adding some texts by authors from other countries. Whenever universities speak of the internationalization of the campus, they usually mean establishing exchange programmes. This is, of course, most laudable. But a truly global curriculum would be entirely different, resulting from a new way of thinking. It would be an approach to texts, ideas and problems which would invert Descartes's process of logic. It would begin with synthesis and apply a universal logic to the analysis of issues. Instead of taking the individual as the point of departure and local concerns as the conclusion, a global agenda should begin with humanity i.e. with all citizens of the world, together with an inclusive peace.

Dear friends,

Thomas Hardy wrote that 'War makes rattling good history; but peace is poor reading,' and Ambrose Bierce described that 'Peace in international affairs is, more often, a period of cheating between two periods of fighting.' Taking into account such pointed remarks, if we wish to promote peace and not violence, we should rewrite history as the story of peace rudely interrupted by war. We need to replace the glorification of war by peace. We need to identify the heroes of pacifism and replace the celebration of militarism by that of non-violence. In fact, do we know who were the architects of peace in the past? We know the names of the generals who fought decisive battles but rarely the names of the signatories of peace accords. Thus, the United Nations would be well advised if asked to publish a history of peace; a new world history in which the artisans of peace are celebrated as heroes and heroines.

Numerous publications during the celebrations of the last centenary included long pages for each year of the twentieth century. On each page figured a litany of disasters, both natural and those caused by us human beings. The sole exception was the moon walk by American astronauts. However, the issue could and should just as easily have listed the accomplishments of humankind: the scientific achievements, the engineering feats, the artistic creations and performances, the architectural dreams which have been realized, the diseases which have been eradicated. Voltaire, in reflecting on history, said that all that would remain of his century would be the scientific and artistic creations. This would have been indeed an excellent heritage for the next generation. The last century left us new discoveries and great achievements which we should celebrate. This is not to say that we should forget the contributions of those who fought for freedom and democracy. We should, however, use history as a lesson and try to infuse in the mind and heart of each scholar the determination that war should never take place again.

Schools are a mirror of society, but the society of tomorrow will be a mirror of our schools today. If we can change the system of education, we can change the world. We can improve the prospects for peace. We can create a climate in which respect, tolerance and generosity of spirit are accepted as desired goals, along with the improved economic status of the individual and society.

We need to espouse as soon as possible a bold, new educational matrix. This is no small experiment but a major revolution in teaching and learning. The means will involve an international commitment and the use of technology to break down the barriers of time, space, economics and culture which separate people. The adoption of technology will represent a significant investment. Yet this will not be the major obstacle. Equipping schools and students around the world, in rich and poor nations alike, will be seen as being to the advantage of one and all. Marketers and consumers, capitalists and leftists alike will support this development. Thus, the means for change will be available.

The real problem will be creating the desire for change, since everyone, each individual, each cultural group, each nation, implicitly realizes the power of education. None wishes to give up control of this source of economic and political power: each neighbourhood wants control of its school. Each linguistic and cultural group wants to create its own learning environment. The provinces want to control the school system and the national governments never fail to place education on the national agenda. An international or global agenda never appears on our radar screens unless UNESCO, OECD, UNDP or the World Bank publish some comparative figures which demonstrate that our students performed on tests exceptionally well or very poorly compared to others around the world. Such has been the case most recently with the OECD's PISA Report, in which the concern is not global but self-centred. We want our workforce to compete favourably. We want our own children to have the best jobs and consequent income.

In order for any educational global agenda to succeed today, the role of education and educators has to be appreciated anew. To start with, we need to respect teachers in order for students to respect the knowledge and values they try to impart. In some countries teachers cannot make a living through teaching. They must supplement their incomes with second jobs in order to survive. In other countries, university professors must teach at several universities or do odd jobs in order to eke out a living. This eliminates the possibility of research. How does one measure the ideas which were not explored, the discoveries and inventions which have not been placed in the service of humankind? In countries which can afford the best, education still suffers. There must be an international recognition of the importance of education and of the significance of the role of the teacher. This is in the interests of each citizen of the globe and of each global citizen alike.

All schools should always be islands of peace, zones where respect and sharing are the rule. All programmes should include at least a second language and the study of the cultures of the world. Every curriculum should include works in which the reader's culture is the subject of a critical view from another culture. Each student should learn to see him or herself from the perspective of other eyes.

An international think tank should be designated to re-imagine and reformulate the way we teach and learn to create a truly global curriculum, since what people ache for today is a vision. The school should be the focal point from which this vision radiates.

Every action, every thought should be in the service of a vision of a world from which violence, intolerance, egoism and ignorance are banished.

In my view, education for peace is not a utopian dream. On the contrary, it is a possibility which does not depend on a single act, a single site, a single school or a single teacher. It can be a reality in every community, in every school. The creation of values and moral certitudes is not dependent on laws or rules but on a huge continuum of small acts which, combined with the human will, can and will succeed. The Berlin Wall crumbled under the weight of the will of the people. There is no stronger force than human will. Such a will must now be employed in taking down instead of building walls; in placing arms in museums instead of planting landmines.

Education occurs not only in the school or in the campus, and not only from nine to five. Education happens every day, all day. Each one of us is an educator, often unwittingly. Each of us is a good or a bad model. Education is not only the responsibility of the teachers or the parents. It is the responsibility of every citizen and must be shared by all. This means that any educational project must radiate far beyond the classroom. It must be a life plan which will be a plan for the future of life on Earth. Totally inclusive, this new world view will enable the grandeur of the human spirit to soar and will make of each of us the architects of one aspect of the future. Each individual is important in coping with the responsibility of each towards the others, of each towards nature, of each towards the future. Our names will be inscribed in the pages of history with shame or content depending on whether or not we have accomplished our duty.

Dear friends,

In closing, let me quote now Samuel Grafton, who said that 'If on a starry night we take the smallest coin in our hand and hold it up in front of our eyes, we will effectively block out half the universe.' The obstacles to a new renaissance for humanity, to a harmonious relationship between mankind and nature, as well as to a new global humanism, seem petty indeed. We must remove the blinkers from our eyes and invest our coins rather in our children (or grandchildren!) in order to grasp a greater vision while building a better future for all.

Such should be the message of our World Academy around the world!

Thank you.

Madrid, November 2005

Glossary

Adenauer, Konrad Hermann Josef (1876–1967), German statesman; imprisoned twice by Nazis during Second World War; first chancellor of West Germany (1949–63) .

Attitude of unilateral hegemony Hegemony: a power attained by defeating others. In this context, the effect upon other countries of the US economy, armaments, culture and intelligence; especially used to criticize US military operations against other countries.

Basque ETA (Euskadi Ta Askatasuna) Basque Homeland and Freedom, Basque radical nationalist organization founded in 1959 for independence from Spain.

Bergson, Henri Louis (1859–1941), French philosopher, awarded the Nobel Prize in Literature and the légion d'honneur.

Betancur, Belisario (1923–), Colombian statesman, former president of Colombia (1982–6); initiated peace talks with several Colombian guerrilla groups and crusades against drugs.

Ceremony in the Air The second of the three assemblies described in the Lotus Sutra in which the entire gathering is suspended in space above the ground; expresses the true aspect of life that the Buddha realized.

Chowdhury, Anwarul K. (1943–) Bangladeshi ambassador to the United Nations, the United Nations under-secretary-general; had heavy responsibility in the United Nations Security Council and Economic and Social Council.

Club of Rome A private organization founded by world intellectuals in 1968 to study measures to address the global problems of environment, population, food and energy.

Coudenhove-Kalergi, Richard (1894–1972) founded the Pan-european Movement to unite all European states into one political body; author of *Pan-Europa* (1923).

Cousins, Norman (1915–90), American essayist and *Saturday Review* editor, co-authored *Dialogue Between Citizens of the World* (1991, in Japanese) with Daisaku Ikeda.

Dinoflagellates Unicellular protists with two flagella; some are photosynthetic and swim by swirling their flagella.

Don Quixote A novel by Miguel de Cervantes Saavedra (1547–1616); the hero Don Quixote sees windmills as monsters that he attacks, and from this episode dreamy and idealistic persons are compared to Don Quixote.

Earth Charter Global consensus statement on fundamental principles for building a just, sustainable and peaceful global society for the twenty-first century, endorsed by over 2,400 organizations, including global institutions such as UNESCO and the World Conservation Union.

Enlightenment for Women The view of T'ien T'ai of China was that by means of the sutras before the Lotus Sutra, women could never attain Buddhahood, but with the Dragon Girl's enlightenment in the Devadatta (twelfth) chapter of the Lotus Sutra, female enlightenment was proved possible for the first time.

Era of humane competition Tsunesaburo Makiguchi (1871–1944) prophesied in his *A Geography of Human Life* (1903) that the epochs of military, political and economic competition will be superseded by one of humane competition.

Ethical relativism The idea that ethical bases differ according to age and social customs, consequently no one can decide whether a particular ethical basis is right or not; a generous idea but dangerous to apply in every instance.

European Union An organization to promote economic and political integration organized by the Treaty on European Union (Maastricht Treaty) in 1993.

Five major Buddhist precepts The basic precepts to be observed by laypersons: (1) not to kill; (2) not to steal; (3) not to engage in sexual misconduct; (4) not to lie; and (5) not to consume intoxicants.

Four leading Bodhisattvas The four leaders of the Bodhisattvas of the Earth described in the 'Emerging from the Earth' (fifteenth) chapter of the Lotus Sutra: Superior Practices, Boundless Practices, Pure Practices and Firmly Established Practices.

Franco regime (1939–75) autocratic political administration under Francisco Franco (1892–1975) after Franco's victory in the Spanish Civil War (1936–9).

Gaia In the late 1960s James E. Lovelock (1919–), British chemist, proposed the Gaia hypothesis that living and nonliving parts of the earth are a complex, interacting system that functions as a single organism. In this context, the Earth is struck by illnesses such as global warming and ocean pollution .

Gaulle, Charles André Joseph Marie de (1890–1970) French Résistance leader against Nazi Germany during Second World War; French president (1958–69).

Gender Acquired social and cultural sexual role and limitation.

Global governance A concept to resolve conflicts between countries independently without relying on global government;

process or framework to resolve global problems by citizens, non-governmental organizations, etc., to smooth the conflicts of interest of the countries.

Global primary-education fund The international framework for collection of funds to promote primary education proposed by Daisaku Ikeda in his 2004 peace proposal, 'Inner Transformation: Creating a Global Groundswell for Peace'.

Globalization Political, economic and cultural expansion on a global scale originated by the development of information and transportation technologies .

Gorbachev, Mikhail S. (1931–) statesman and the last president of the USSR; his political reforms led to the end of the Cold War and also the dissolution of the USSR; awarded the Nobel Peace Prize (1990).

El Hassan bin Talal, Prince of Jordan (1947–), the former president of the Club of Rome and the supreme adviser to the European Academy of Sciences and Arts; exercises leadership, especially in the fields of peace, human rights and education .

Hegemonic power The power of the conqueror, obtained through maintaining the superiority and leadership of one's own country independently by making use of political, cultural, economic and military advantages.

Hugo, Victor (1802–85) French poet, novelist and dramatist, criticized the coup d'état of Charles Louis Napoléon Bonaparte and lived in self-imposed exile for nineteen years.

Innate good and innate evil The idea that human beings are gifted by nature with innate good and, on the other hand, the idea that human beings possess innate evil.

Jaspers, Karl (1883–1969) German psychiatrist and philosopher.

Juan Carlos I of Spain (1938–) enthroned after the death of Francisco Franco, initiated democratic reforms notwithstanding opposition by old domestic powers, regarded as the symbol of Spain's unity.

Jung, Carl Gustav (1875–1961) Swiss psychiatrist and thinker; founder of analytical psychology, posited the common existence of a collective unconscious under the individual subconsciousnesses of all people.

Kant, Immanuel (1724–1804) German philosopher and scientist; author of *Critique of Pure Reason*.

Kennedy, Edward Moore (1932–), youngest brother of John F. Kennedy; US Senator of Massachusetts.

Kennedy, John Fitzgerald (1917–63), thirty-fifth President of the USA (1961–3); his administration faced challenges such as the Cuban Missile Crisis, the building of the Berlin Wall and the Vietnam War.

Knight Grand Cross of Rizal The Order of the Knights of Rizal in the Philippines honours those who act in the spirit of José Rizal (1861–96), the national hero of the Philippines' independence movement.

Gandhi, Mohandas Karamchand, 'Mahatma Ghandi' (1869–1948) leader of the Indian nationalist movement against British rule, esteemed for his doctrine of non-violent protest, Mahatma is a designation meaning 'Great Soul'.

Makiguchi, Tsunesaburo (1871–1944) educator, founder-president of the Soka Gakkai and author of *Education for Creative Living* and *A Geography of Human Life*; opposed war. Imprisoned by the Japanese military government during Second World War, died in prison.

Malraux, André (1901–76) French writer and critic; French minister of intelligence and culture, author of *La condition humaine*.

Media literacy Ability to read information adequately and not be influenced by mass media like television, newspapers, advertisements, etc.

Militaristic indoctrination In this context, the efforts by the Japanese military government to promote war through education during Second World War.

Nazism Political ideas or systems of the National Socialist German Workers' Party founded in 1919, commonly called the Nazi Party, especially intolerant nationalism and totalitarianism; Adolf Hitler (1889–1945), the party's leader, was appointed chancellor of Germany in 1933.

Non-aligned nations During the Cold War period between the Communist East and the democratic West, many nations considered themselves not formally aligned with or against any major power bloc.

North Atlantic Treaty Organization (NATO) An international military organization for collaboration on defence; established in 1949 by twelve countries; the treaty states that an attack on one signatory will be regarded as an attack on all signatories, and that the signatories must counterattack in cooperation .

Nuclear threat Nuclear powers develop and stockpile nuclear weapons sufficient to annihilate human beings many times over, to the extent that the people of the world now face the danger of extinction by nuclear weapons.

Nyerere, Julius (1922–99) first president of Tanzania, father of Tanzanian independence.

Organization of American States (OAS) a regional multilateral forum to strengthen cooperation on democratic values, defend common interests and debate the major issues facing the region and the world; made up of thirty-five member states in North, Central and South America and the Caribbean.

Peace Constitution The Constitution of Japan has been called the Peace Constitution; its preamble confirms that all peoples of the world have the right to live in peace; Article 9 renounces the right to wage war.

Peccei, Aurelio (1908–84) entrepreneur and economist, took an active part in the resistance movement during Second World War, founded the Club of Rome (1968).

Power games Race for power; especially struggles by superpowers for hegemony in international society against background of political and economic power.

Prometheus A character in Greek mythology; considered the patron of civilization for his bestowal of the gift of fire.

Proposal to the World Summit on Sustainable Development In August 2002, the World Summit for Sustainable Development was held in Johannesburg and Daisaku Ikeda submitted the proposal 'The Challenge of Global Environment: Education for a Sustainable Future'.

Pugwash Conferences on Science and World Affairs International organization of scholars and public figures founded in 1957 by Joseph Rotblat and Bertrand Russell in Pugwash, Canada, to reduce the danger of armed conflict and to seek solutions to global security; Pugwash and Rotblat jointly won the Nobel Peace Prize in 1995 for their efforts towards nuclear disarmament.

Romance languages The generic name of languages developed from Latin, differentiated regionally and formed by the eighth century, now spoken by about 500 million people in Europe and Latin America.

Rusk, Dean (1909–94) American politician, served as secretary of state to the presidencies of J. F. Kennedy and L. B. Johnson.

Sagan, Carl (1934–96) American astronomer; author of *Cosmos* (1980).

Soka Gakkai International (SGI) A Buddhist network in 190 countries and regions that actively promotes peace, culture and education through personal change and social contribution; founded in 1975.

Spanish Civil War The army headed by Francisco Franco rose in revolt against the Popular Front government that won the general election in 1936; the civil war brought chaos to Spain from 1936 to 1939, ended with the victory of Franco's Nationalist troops and with about 500,000 deaths .

Structural violence Concept used by Johan Galtung, Norwegian peace researcher, to describe poverty and oppression in developing countries resulting not only from internal causes but also from international and domestic social and economic systems.

Swaminathan, M. S. (1925–) president of the Pugwash Conferences on Science and World Affairs, chairman of the National Commission on Agriculture, Food, and Nutrition Security of India; winner of the World Food Prize in 1987.

Technoscientific Technoscientific studies examine the decisive role of science and technology in how knowledge is being developed within the social context of science.

Tehranian, Majid (1937–) professor of international communications at the University of Hawaii and director of the Toda Institute for Global Peace and Policy Research; co-author of *Global Civilization, A Buddhist-Islamic Dialogue* (2003) with Daisaku Ikeda.

Ten Commandments The Decalogue; given to Moses on Mount Sinai in the form of two stone tablets; remonstrates against murder, fornication, theft, perjury, etc.

Thoreau, Henry David (1817–62) an American thinker who opposed the Mexican war in 1846 and was imprisoned; his thoughts affected the philosophies and activities of Mahatma Gandhi and Martin Luther King, Jr.

Three virtues of sovereign, teacher, and parent Three virtues that all people should respect; the benevolent functions of sovereign, teacher and parent a Buddha is said to possess: (1) the virtue of sovereign is the power to protect all living beings; (2) the virtue of teacher is the wisdom to instruct and lead all persons to enlightenment; and (3) the virtue of parent is the compassion to nurture and support.

Toda, Josei (1900–58) second president of the Soka Gakkai, a direct disciple of the founding president, Tsunesaburo Makiguchi, and mentor of the third president, Daisaku Ikeda; opposed war and was imprisoned by the Japanese military government during Second World War.

Toynbee, Arnold J. (1889–1975) English historian best known for his twelve-volume *A Study of History* (1934–61); co-author of *Choose Life: A Dialogue* with Daisaku Ikeda.

Treasure Tower A massive stupa adorned with jewels depicted in Buddhist scriptures, specifically in the 'Treasure Tower' chapter (eleventh) of the Lotus Sutra; Nichiren viewed the Treasure Tower as an allegory representing precious human life.

UNESCO The United Nations Educational, Scientific, and Cultural Organization, founded in 1945 to build peace in the minds of people by means of education, the social and natural sciences, culture and communication.

Value-Creating Education Practical theory of pedagogy advocated by Tsunesaburo Makiguchi to develop the talent of those who would create and add value for the happiness of the people.

World Health Organization (WHO) Founded in 1948 with 192 signatories; headquarters in Geneva. It is the directing and coordinating authority for health within the UN system, taking preventive measures against epidemics and working on environmental problems.

Zamenhof, Ludwig Lejzer (1859–1917) Polish oculist and linguist, father of Esperanto, an artificial international language.

Zhou Enlai (1898–1976), Chinese premier (1949–76) who exercised leadership in domestic administration and foreign affairs at the founding of the People's Republic of China.

Zionism Movement to build a Jewish nation in Palestine, started at the end of the nineteenth century in the midst of the rising tide of persecution of Jewish people in Europe.

Notes

Chapter 2

1 Henry David Thoreau, *Walden and Civil Disobedience* (Penguin Books, New York, 1983), p. 398.
2 Nichiren, *The Record of the Orally Transmitted Teachings*, trans. Burton Watson (Soka Gakkai, Tokyo, 2004), p. 138.

Chapter 3

1 Tsunesaburo Makiguchi, *A Geography of Human Life* (Caddo Gap Press, San Francisco, 2002), p. 25.
2 Nichiren, *The Writings of Nichiren Daishonin* (Soka Gakkai, Tokyo, 1999), p. 119.
3 Miguel de Cervantes, *The Adventures of Don Quixote*, trans. J. M. Cohen (Penguin Books, London, 1950), p. 583.
4 The exhibition opened at the UN headquarters in 1982 before beginning a world tour.

Chapter 5

1 Nichiren, *Writings of Nichiren Daishonin*, p. 644.
2 Alan AtKisson, *Believing Cassandra: An Optimist Looks at a Pessimist's World* (Chelsea Green Publishing Company, White River Jct, 1999), p. 73.
3 Aurelio Peccei and Daisaku Ikeda, *Before It Is Too Late*, ed. Richard L. Gage (Kodansha International, Tokyo, 1984), p. 131.

Chapter 9

1 'When a nation becomes disordered, it is the spirits that first show signs of rampancy. Because the spirits become rampant,

all the people of the nation become disordered.' (Nichiren, *Writings of Nichiren Daishonin*, p. 8)

2 Address at American University, Washington, DC, 10 June 1963.

3 Carl Gustav Jung, *Gegenwart und Zukunft*, (1957).

Chapter 10

1 Norman Cousins, *Human Options* (W.W. Norton Company, New York, 1981), p. 30.

Chapter 11

1 Karl Jaspers, *Vom Ursprung und Ziel der Geschichte* (Artemis, Zurich, 1949), p. 46.

2 Norman Cousins, *Present Tense: An American Editor's Odyssey* (McGraw-Hill, New York, 1967).

3 Carl Sagan, *Cosmos* (reissued Ballantine Books, New York, 1985), p. 286.

4 Carl Sagan, *Cosmic Connection: An Extraterrestrial Perspective* (Cambridge University Press, Cambridge, 2000), p. 220.

Chapter 12

1 Nichiren, *Writings of Nichiren Daishonin*, 'On Establishing the Correct Teaching for the Peace of the Land', p. 24.

2 Nichiren, *The Writings of Nichiren Daishonin II* (Soka Gakkai, Tokyo, 2006), p. 931.

Appendix 1

1 Luis Díez del Corral, *El rapto de Europa* (Revista de Occidente, Madrid, 1954), p. 286.

2 Ibid., p. 324.

3 Johann Wolfgang von Goethe, *Faust*, trans. Stuart Atkins (Suhrkamp/Insel, Boston, 1984), Part One, III, p. 40.

4 José Ortega y Gasset, *La rebelión de las masas* (Revolt of the Masses) (Alianza Editorial, Madrid, 1983), p. 74.

5 Hajime Nakamura (trans.), *Budda no shinri no kotoba, kankyo no kotoba* (Buddha's Words of Truth and Inspiration) (Iwanami Shoten, Tokyo, 1978), p. 32.

6 Yoshiro Tamura (trans.), *Ningensei no hakken Hannyakyo* (Discovery of Humanity, the Nirvana Sutra), Vol. 7 of *Gendaijin*

no Bukkyo (Buddhism for Modern People) (Chikuma Shobo, Tokyo, 1966), p. 46.

7   Fumio Masutani, *Bukkyo hyakuwa* (A Hundred Tales of Buddhism), (Chikuma Shobo, Tokyo, 1971), p. 159.

8   Ramón Menéndez Pidal, *Los espanoles en la historia* (Espasa-Calpe, Colección Austral, Madrid, 1991), p. 83.

9   Goethe, *Faust*, 'Night', p. 15.

10 Nichiren, *Writings of Nichiren Daishonin*, p. 644.

11 José Ortega y Gasset, *Meditaciones del Quijote* (Alianza Editorial, Madrid, 1987), p. 25.

12 Ortega y Gasset, *La rebelión de las masas*, p. 100.

13 Miguel de Unamuno, *En tornoal casticismo* (Espasa-Calpe, Madrid, 1961), p.46.

14 Mikhail Gorbachev and Daisaku Ikeda, *Moral Lessons of the Twentieth Century* (I.B.Tauris, London, 2005), p. 18.

15 Ortega y Gasset, *La rebelión de las masas*, p. 118.

16 Philip B. Yampolsky (ed.), Burton Watson et al. (trans.), *Letters of Nichiren* (Columbia University Press, New York, 1996), p. 57.

17 Ibid., pp. 159–60.

18 Ibid., p. 207.

19 Ortega y Gasset, *La rebelión de las masas*, p. 54.

20 Cervantes, *Don Quixote*.

Index